# WHAT THE F*CK!

Because Life Is Full Of Those Moments Where Only These Three Words Will Do!

## JO GILBERT

## DISCLAIMER

This book is full of swearing and profanities (I abbreviate the F-bomb Fucking to Fkn a lot it's not a typo). If you don't like swearing please don't read it, get offended and then leave a review saying it was full of swearing, I know I wrote it that way on purpose!

Also please don't bother writing a review saying she could have used less swearing, well yes I could have but then it wouldn't be written in my authentic voice, would it?

All names used in the book are made up, except my friend's names!

This book is probably not for you if you are easily offended and cannot accept a difference of opinion from someone else without inciting hatred and anger.

We all see life through different lenses, I do not expect you to see life through my lens you have your own. In this book, I am merely sharing a view from my lens, not yours. No single view in the world even if we were in the same place at the same time would ever be the same and that is why we all deserve to be seen and heard, together as a single human race.

Life would be fucking boring otherwise!

It's all a bit tongue-in-cheek, to be honest.

# WHAT F*CKS PEOPLE COULD ACTUALLY GIVE ABOUT THIS BOOK

"Your book is bloody marvellous and I loved its speed, how carefree it feels and how you have just lobbed it at them. And told them to laugh or leave.... Which is precisely the attitude you are encouraging in others."

— KATIE HOPKINS

"This book is brilliant!

It made me pause for a minute and reflect that if you are carrying on when things are so shitty so can I. So, thank you for that.

I think in summary, evoking all the fuckery around us, makes you reflect more on the things we glaze over because as you correctly say we are now conditioned that way.

And for a mild swearer with Presbyterian parents, I felt given permission to justify my swearing!

Absolutely glorious and a book I didn't know I needed but certainly did and so does the world.

Thank you. It's been a pleasure to read it."

— LEAH TRUEMAN, LAUNDRY BUSTER

 "I couldn't put it down! I have literally read it all in one sitting and belly-laughed the entire way through. You have created a masterpiece that just says what we are all thinking and are too British to say.

You're amazing!!"

— EMMA CLAYTON, TEAM, CULTURE AND
COMMUNICATIONS CONSULTANT
BRILLIANT TEAMS LTD

"I have just finished the book, and I have to say it's brilliant. It really had me laughing out loud, it made me mad in some bits and think in others.

The best way I can describe my experience of reading it is, it's like putting the world to rights with a mate over a glass of wine. You share your views agree or disagree, you have a light-hearted debate and you come away feeling lighter. Which is funny when technically it's a one-way conversation, but because it gets you agreeing, disagreeing, laughing, reflecting etc it feels like a conversation. I hope that makes sense."

— TAMMY GREEN, BUSINESS CREATION COACH

"You're a fkn superstar, honestly, I haven't belly-laughed and cried tears like that since Peter Kay - it is gold!!! I have even screenshot bits to go back to and giggle again!! Honestly, I'm humbled that you have let me read it first. It's so good."

— LUCY RENNIE, LR COMMS

"What the F*CK! is genius. It literally made me laugh so hard throughout the entire book. I absolutely love how Jo has bought in facts and makes you think about certain topics. I resonate with most of what has been written (I even realised I might be declared a Cock Womble at one point 😂) Brilliant, Witty and Hilarious! Jo has literally said what we are all thinking, called all the sh*t out and been extremely honest - Love it, a book that should have been written years ago!"

— LOUISA WILLCOX DIRECTOR OF LOUISA WILLCOX: MONEY COACH

"WHAT THE F*CK REVIEW 5★

BLOODY BRILLIANT! Jo says what 'most' of us have been thinking and isn't afraid to ruffle a few feathers in her delivery. If you're having a bad day pick up this book, serious laugh-out-loud moments! Be warned NOT for the faint-hearted or society snowflakes."

— NAOMI HOLBROOK, HEALTH & WELL-BEING TRANSFORMATION COACH WELLTHY EVOLUTION

"What a woman, what a book!

This has to be the BEST book I have ever read!!!

Hilariously funny from start to finish; just thinking about it makes me smile from ear to ear.

The book is filled with a filter-free view of how we unconsciously think and act about business and life. OMG, Jo's resilience is like no other. This book is just what everyone needs: a bloody good laugh."

— HELEN MCCUE, MOMENTS CANDLE COMPANY

**"**

# A smile is a facelift that's in everyone's price range!

TOM WILSON

**"**

## DEDICATION

*To the lovely person who is reading this book right now, yes you, if you have ever experienced those WTF thoughts, you are not alone.*

*People are fkn rude, ridiculously stupid and sometimes complete morons is it any wonder we WTF at them?*

*I am dedicating this book to you, for not losing your absolute shit.*

*I salute you!*

**"**

# Do not take life too seriously. You will never get out of it alive.

– ELBERT HUBBARD

**"**

# CONTENTS

> **66**
>
> # Jo may be the only woman on the planet that can make me sound like a Sunday school teacher.
>
> KATIE HOPKINS
>
> **99**

# FOREWORD

## Katie Hopkins

There are many reasons to love Jo Gilbert and this book, 'What the F*ck!'

It's not just that you can literally hear her voice as you read; her laughter, her attitude and her frustration with those who need to be introduced to their own reflection in a mirror.

And it's not simply because she swears harder than a sailor on a shitty sea, though she does. Jo may be the only woman on the planet that can make me sound like a Sunday school teacher.

But the truth of it is that she's a really good woman, a darn good mother and a wonderful piece of work. I know, very personally, that if you tripped and fell, Jo would swear for you, pick you up and tell you no one saw. Or that your knickers looked great blowing in the breeze. And she would make you laugh even as you cried.

What the fuck IS the moment you take off your bra and jiggle your boobs after a long hot day somewhere you really don't want to be.

Read this book. And love her as I do.

https://www.katiesarms.com/

https://www.instagram.com/_katie_hopkins_/?hl=en

## INTRODUCTION

Hello, my fellow WTF'er.

I love that you are here and are going to come on this journey with me as I share some of life's;

 "what the fuck"

"what the actual fuck"

"what the fucking fuck"

"what in gods name for fuck's sake"

"fuckity fuck fuck"

"oh just fuck off'"

"What a fucking cockwomble"

"Prick"

"Knob jockey"

"what a load of old bollocks"

"Fuck my life"

"Fuck my actual life"

"Are you being fucking serious?"

"Are you actually fucking joking?"

"Are you fucking kidding me?"

"C U Next Tuesday"

"You must be fucking joking"

"What in the glorious fuck are you talking about?!?"

Moments!

I think that sets the tone for the book. Sorry if your phrase is missing.

Allow me to introduce myself, I am Jo Gilbert, a 51-year-old, loyal, clever as fuck (confident as fuck too by all accounts), introverted extrovert. I'm a wife, mum, nani, little sister, best friend, and colleague. I'm also a pretty bloody awesome businesswoman and a No1 best-selling author four times over (maybe five if this one sells enough copies who knows!).

There's no real harm in me, I swear a lot but let's be honest here, who doesn't except my friend Shaz? She literally never swears a single word I adore how she can get through life without the odd WHAT THE FUCK spurting out. I would absolutely die laughing if I ever heard Shaz say it.

I'll be honest I swear enough for ten people so there is balance. I do however have a profanity filter, which engages when I'm working with a client or in front of my mum, not a single F word pops out!

I hate no one and love hard. I value others' opinions and a good debate without prejudice and hate. Some people do however irritate the shit out of me and do cause me to frequently mutter under my breath *'oh just fuck off'*. Being irritated by someone is not the same as hatred. I think hatred incitement is everything that is wrong with society today.

Some people, of course, I just think are fkn idiots and should not be let out of the house without supervision.

I describe a lot of the people who irritate me in the pages of this book. If you recognise yourself, in general amongst them, then perhaps stop being a twat, no one likes a twat!

I've experienced some unbelievable shit in my life, which I've already written a book about in 2018 called "Strength & Power" you should go read it, it is full of adversity and shit, FML I'm surprised I'm still here. That book describes the shitstorm that has been and to be honest continues to be my life.

Did I mention yet my three divorces and four husbands? No? Well, you can imagine why I swear a lot! One husband is enough for anyone never mind four of the fuckers! What can I say, I either like a good wedding, the cake, and variety or I'm a fkn glutton for punishment! I'm not sure which.

 "I love being married. It's so great to find that one special person you want to annoy for the rest of your life."

— RITA RUDNER

Have you ever been on a rollercoaster, like the '*Pepsi Max*' at Blackpool Please Beach, front row seat, it's not bad is it on the way up, then whoosh, FML, whoosh here we go, then slowly, slowly climb, then fucking hell stop the fucking ride I want to get off. Well, that's how my life has felt at times, one great big long ride on a white knuckle rollercoaster which I never signed up for.

At 51 years old I do wonder when the ride is going to stop, I'll hear someone say 'you can get off now and go and enjoy some candy floss and chuck a coconut at the targets to win a goldfish.' Although I doubt it will stop (until I naturally pop my clogs), hence my collection of phrases to get me through everyday life.

These are my genuine WTF moments and thoughts. I make no apologies for them. I am guilty of doing some of them too!

I hope you enjoy the book and read it with the light-hearted intent it was written. Think Nan by Catherine Tate and Miriam Margoyles as you read it, I will never be as funny as them, however, I am becoming more like them as I grow older. It has been one of the most enjoyable experiences of my life, just writing about everything (well most things at least) that pisses me off.

Enjoy!

*With much love and fun*
*Jo xx*

"

# I don't give offence you choose to take it

KATIE HOPKINS

"

# SCAM ARTISTS, FRAUDSTERS & JOKERS

## FRAUDSTERS

 "What the fuck! If I ever find that woman, I will drag her skanky arse to jail."

I need to get this one out of the way first and then lighten the mood.

These are the strong words of sheer frustration and anger bellowing from my mouth, every time I think about the con woman who was living and working as an estate agent in Lanzarote, who played me for a mug with a long con.

It has all the makings of a Netflix documentary!

This my friend is the biggest financial WHAT THE ACTUAL FUCK moment of my life.

In August 2018 I was what is known as *'long conned'* whilst purchasing a villa in Lanzarote by an unscrupulous estate agent and her client. Although I wasn't fully aware of the enormity of her fraudulent ways until December 2021.

Let's fast forward to then, where it transpired she was preying on British and European ex-pats and stealing their properties and life savings of over €3 million. Not just in Lanzarote, victims of her fraud have come forward from Fuerteventura and Gran Canaria, and the scale of her theft is still rising.

There is now an international red warrant out for her arrest. I don't believe for one minute she is living a lavish lifestyle, you see the sad thing in all of this is that she was apparently a coke, alcohol and gambling addict. She hasn't got a pot to piss in, because during lockdowns, living alone, she gambled every single cent of the money she stole on online bingo, or so the radio, newspapers and Facebook groups looking for her are reporting.

All of that hurt, so many families and she has nothing to show for it, she didn't just destroy others' lives she destroyed her own and when she is caught will probably spend the rest of her life in prison.

The story we were sold was one of sadness, family loss, bereavement and heartbreak, a sad situation we should be patient with whilst complex inheritance issues were resolved, it would take no more than 3 months - *'just trust me everything will be ok'*, she said, fuck my life!!!

We agreed to buy a villa for a confirmed and accepted purchase price of €300k. We paid a deposit and moved in, handing €225k over in the months that followed. We had a small mortgage approved and then never got the title deeds confirming we owned the property signed and witnessed by the notary. Excuse after excuse followed always to do with inheritance issues she was sorting out for her client.

She jumped bail in December 2021 following a court case for another property fraud she had been brought to court for, that's the first I knew she was more rotten than we thought she was. The court didn't take her passport, and she vanished, with at least €150k of the money we had paid. The owner of the villa claims he has only ever received €75k, oddly the court is finding it impossible to locate him too.

I am now left suing the owner (if we can ever find him), as she was his agent, not mine and his trusted general power of attorney, confirmed by him in writing as having rights to sell his property to us. We do have a purchase contract and possession of the villa which by the way, we no longer fkn want because of everything that's happened. I don't care how lovely the villa is, I'd rather live in a tent now than somewhere that is a constant reminder of this shit show every day!

I may never see a penny of that money ever again, I can't sell the villa, because on paper at the notary I don't legally own it, we are in limbo. I remain hopeful and whilst there's a fight in me I will continue to fight for what is legally mine. Although the strain it puts on you mentally every day is an absolute mind fuck!

I'm sorry if you know me and are discovering this for the first time. Lanzarote has been the worst 4.5 years of my life! I have tried so hard to hide it from social media, as I know so many of you want to live the sunshine dream too. So I've smiled through the river of mental shit I trudge through daily.

Total financial **losses** to date for a move abroad are circa €355,000 and rising with the legal costs and additional interest costs of £65k on a mortgage we wouldn't have needed if this hadn't of happened. It's a life changing sum of money.

A crook is too kind a word to use for her. I have many choice words, the very thought of them both brings out the worst in me. I will have my moment one day when she is brought to justice and this court case is over.

Yes, I'm still laughing and smiling, I'm still alive, I'm still happy, and I still have my health, although please refer to chapter 11, I have more to say on health.

I'm still earning, and I'm still supporting people in business every day in many ways - it's what I do. I just get on with it, there is no point in me crying over this shit show every day, it isn't going to change what has already happened, but I can influence today and my future.

So fraudsters are high on up there in the WTF scale for me. They are simply described as entitled narcissistic low lives.

I'm going to award this one a;

 *"what a fucking shower of shit."* 💩💩💩

## SCAM TEXT MESSAGES

When the government provide grants for energy bills or council tax relief or HMRC has a rebate for you. For the love of god, please don't fall for these scammy text messages.

The post office, DPD, Hermes, or FedEx - you have missed a delivery text message click this link to track your parcel - don't do it!

Don't go claiming your rebate from fake HMRC text messages always go to them directly and never ever click these messages or similar ones from your bank or building society.

Text Message
Today 19:19

HMRC Refund: You have an outstanding Tax refund of £276.74 from 2020 to 2021. Follow instructions to claim your Tax refund at: https://gov-tax.refundpr.com/

If you do find yourself clicking these links, *'WTF you absolute cockwomble, what are you thinking Linda for fucks sake!'*

I'm awarding text messages two things

To the scammer - *you fucking lowlife scumbag*

To you - *you cockwomble for clicking it*

## SCAM EMAILS / PHISHING

Scores on the WTF scale - *'Oh just fuck off'.*

If you receive emails from any financial organisations asking you via email to click the link - that is an immediate RED FLAG do not click it. In the 'From' section of the email on your phone or email software, Click on the sender, gary298529529HMRC@gmail.con as an example pops up, it's really easy to spot.

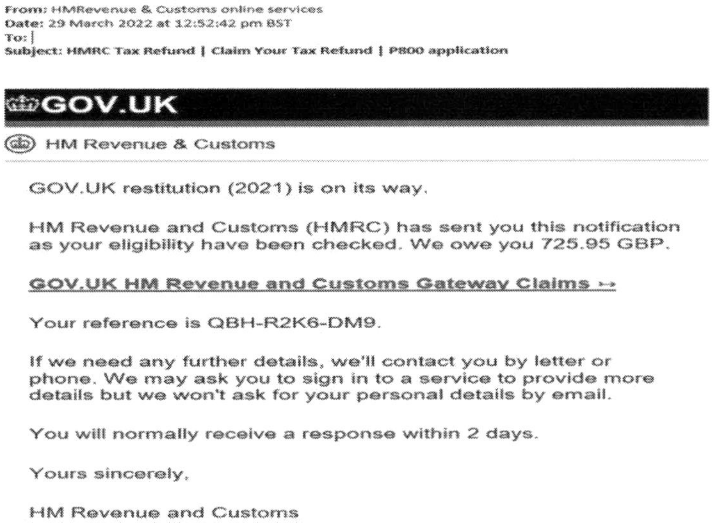

**From:** HMRevenue & Customs online services
**Date:** 29 March 2022 at 12:52:42 pm BST
**To:**
**Subject:** HMRC Tax Refund | Claim Your Tax Refund | P800 application

GOV.UK

HM Revenue & Customs

GOV.UK restitution (2021) is on its way.

HM Revenue and Customs (HMRC) has sent you this notification as your eligibility have been checked. We owe you 725.95 GBP.

GOV.UK HM Revenue and Customs Gateway Claims →

Your reference is QBH-R2K6-DM9.

If we need any further details, we'll contact you by letter or phone. We may ask you to sign in to a service to provide more details but we won't ask for your personal details by email.

You will normally receive a response within 2 days.

Yours sincerely,

HM Revenue and Customs

If in doubt don't click the link, always go to the originator's website or phone them. Clearly don't phone any of the numbers from an email or text message you've received.

If you do, well I'd be thinking you are a Cockwomble. There is still hope for you it's an awareness thing, you can recover from Cockwomblism. Just use your common sense Linda FFS!

## PHONE CALL SCAMMERS

Fuck my actual life, I swear to god if Jason from Microsoft in London, sounding like he just fell from an Indian call centre night shift phones me one more time I'm going to scream.

I've got more blocked numbers on my phone than contacts!

If you receive a call advising you that your internet security is compromised, asking you to go to a website and click a link and you actually do it, then my friend, I hate to tell you this, but you really are fucking stupid!

Taking advantage of stupid people - scores a 'are *you are fkn joking me?'* wow you actually fell for it.

## CHARITY SCAMMERS

Allow me to set the scene for you.

Sheila is out shopping in town, minding her own business enjoying a leisurely stroll browsing past shop windows, bobbing in and out of the shops.

Incoming is a 16-25 year old with a clipboard. They are blocking Sheila's path and waving a badge and board in her face.

'Hi, how are you today, look at the puppy, look at the puppppeeeee" next minute she's given her bank details away on a charity raffle for a charity she's never even heard of.

With a quick flash of a badge, she had no time to read or validate and it was too late, Sheila has signed her life savings over.

For fuck's sake Sheila, just say no. Be firm and if they persist just tell them to 'fuck off'. Give to charity when you are ready, not when you are pressured to whilst trying to enjoy your morning off from the kids and your husband farting on the sofa. You don't even know if they are scammers or not, why risk it?

If you want to give to charity again go to the charity's official website to do it - FFS, can you see the theme here? Do not stop to chat, do not pass go or allow them to collect your £200, just go into Primark Sheila, and remember why you came uptown in the first place! Little Billy needs a school uniform and it's nearly Christmas, save your money, Sheila!

On your list of things to do, it didn't say; give a complete stranger twenty quid and my bank details did it? Come on Sheila, for god's sake smell the coffee.

Some registered charities do sign you up in this way - I fundamentally disagree with it, to me, it's pressure sales, it doesn't sit right with me, and it doesn't mean you have to agree with me. I think volunteers who are raising funds are doing a great job, but there is a time and a place and hassling people in the street is not one of them.

Just please be careful giving your bank details out to complete strangers in the street.

Also while we are on the subject, how annoying are those tub and bucket shakers outside Asda and Tesco (other supermarkets are available) who smile and shake their plastic shit at you and give you the guilt and death stare.

WTF, do they have any idea how intimidating it is to shake a bucket in people's faces, especially the face of someone who never carries cash on them? For the love of god, I came in for a pint of milk I've got a debit card only and you are hassling me for two quid, just fuck off!

Charity scammers, I rank you as the lowest form of life form *just fuck off.*

People with buckets - *'Are you fucking kidding me?'*

## CASH MACHINE AND CARD CLONING

In December 2017, my credit card was cloned. I have no idea how or where. On boxing day, £4500 disappeared from my account, and on the 3rd of January, another

£4500 was spent, on both occasions in the Microsoft online store.

I had no idea as I was celebrating Christmas, the New Year and my birthday, it's always a big week for me. It was only on the 3rd attempt of another £4500 on the 7th of January that the MBNA credit card fraud team contacted me.

It didn't cost me anything in the end, but my card was frozen along with my credit line while this was investigated.

A few days later a personal coach from Australia who really should have known better took almost £1700 from my debit card. I didn't out him for it on social media, I perhaps should have warned others in my network about him. Instead, my email to him clearly stated the fkn stupid mistake he'd made and that he had been reported to the police and bank fraud team. I didn't get my money back and never heard from him again.

He had saved my card details over the phone when I paid him for a coaching session 3 months earlier. No contract in place, nothing, and without warning, he debited the funds and flew off on his holiday to the Maldives. I was fuming. I was about to fly to Singapore and then on to Bali and I was so angry with him and the bank for allowing it, that I closed my account in temper. I lost my upgrade to Business Class on our flight out to Singapore as my pre-registered card with the airline failed. Fucking livid I was, a proper angry little gnome.

On our flight now in economy class a week later, I proceeded to accidentally chuck a cup full of red wine all over my best mate Abi. I got passed two apples by the stewardess, god knows why, it was pitch black dark, I was a few drinks in and confused at the passing of the apple.

Abi was sleeping so I saw what I thought was an empty cup on the cupholder of the seat in front of her and dropped the apple in it, when I say drop, it was more like a slam dunk. Big mistake, fucking huge mistake actually, it was full to the brim with red wine she hadn't drunk. A full cup of wine on a flight to me is unheard of, like what the actual fuck, so you can imagine my shock.

She was wearing all white, she was livid. She looked like I had knifed her, and I was that friend who just pissed myself laughing. I was quite tipsy because like a normal person, I had actually drunk my wine when it was served to me. I grabbed the only dry blanket we had between us and mopped up the drink with it. I then proceeded to lay back and go to sleep, leaving her in her newly stained white wet clothes.

So yeah debit and credit card fraudsters and people who save your card details without permission and take money from your accounts, you get an '*are you being fucking seri-*

*ous? fuck, fuck, FUCK,* you bunch of *C U Next Tuesdays!'*

## CLIENTS WHO DON'T PAY

Here we go, I wasn't going to go here but here I am. 100%, I think you are a low life if you have taken services from someone, ordered goods from someone, whatever it is where there was an agreement in place for an exchange of money for the product or service that you received and then you decided not to pay, skip payments or pay when you feel like it (the worst!).

For clarity, I am not talking about people who experience a change in circumstances unexpectedly e.g. redundancy or loss of a loved one.

Here's what the law has to say!

> **It is an offence for a defendant to obtain, by any dishonest act, services for which payment is required, with intent to avoid payment for those services under the Fraud Act 2006 (FrA 2006).**

You are no different to all of the previous scammers I've mentioned. Theft is theft, let's not dress this up here.

When you don't pay your business coach, or for your Etsy order, or eBay order or you reverse refund a PayPal payment for goods and services you have received, in my mind you are a scammer.

If you have asked for a payment plan for a course and after a few months decided fuck it I'll stop paying or just pay whenever I feel like it, or keep promising to pay on Monday but then don't, expect to find yourself in the small claims court!

People rely on your word that you will pay what you owe, they also have families to feed and bills to pay too. If you can't afford these things then don't fucking buy them. No excuses just fucking stop it!

On the WTF scale, you are a *'fucking knob jockey'* you need to sort your entitled life out.

———

Let me be clear here, clients who don't pay are not the same group of people as clients who buy something and then feel ripped off, mis-sold and misled, so stop paying.

This is for all the Sheilas of this world. If this has happened to you, you may be entitled to a refund and you can take your case to trading standards and small claims court.

Please read the small print in your contract if you have one, or the terms and conditions of the sale. Do your due diligence and ask people who have already done the courses or used the services you are intending to buy. I strongly advise that you don't go asking paid affiliates as there is clearly a conflict of interest here, they are getting paid to sell you something for a third party.

Although most Bizness Coaches and small Biznesses (FML the cheese of it all!) do not tell you what your rights are regarding refunds, disputes, where to get help when you struggle to pay, or what their complaints procedure is, they should have this documented and you can request a copy. Depending on whether you have purchased goods or services from them on a B2B or B2C basis the protection you have in place is slightly different.

Please ensure you know which type of consumer you are before entering into agreements to purchase and know your rights. Also, ask to see a copy of their complaints procedure in case things go wrong, if they don't have one or fail to produce one then this is a red flag you shouldn't be ignoring.

You should also know or ask for their privacy policy (not their website privacy policy, their company privacy policy regarding how they will handle your data and keep the contract between you both confidential and not plastered all over Facebook when things go wrong (they are two different things).

You have never once seen a company like Vodafone plaster their annoyance at you all over Facebook by being obscure enough not to identify you but everyone in their networks knows who they mean and then get their loyal fanbase to come and give you a good dosing down online so you feel unprotected and attacked.

A professional would never do this!

You are protected via the Consumer Rights Act 2015. You can get help and support with complaints and if you are struggling to pay via the Citizens Advice Bureau.

## COACHES AND OTHER 'ONLINE BIZNESSES'

There are certain people online who have set themselves up as 'BIZness coaches' offering the dream of £10k, £50k, sod it lets go £100k plus months if you work with them (try saying 'High Ticket' in a camp welsh accent, its about as close to cheesy as this gets).

We can refer to these people mostly as "Pandemic Coaches".

They charge ridiculous amounts of money to join group coaching programmes or 1-2-1 packages and then deliver the biggest load of shite you've ever seen or heard. In my mind, they charge B2B prices to B2C consumers with no regulation on what is fair in terms of value for money and pricing. BUYERS BEWARE!!!

The sales patter and constant barrage on your Facebook news feed of oh look at me, be like me, join my gang, the sales funnel, the constant stream of nonsense time sensitive emails with made-up gushing and woo words.

All targeting Sheila again! The poor cow has already bought herself a new puppy she didn't want and now she's about to sign over all of her Christmas savings to buy a course in the hope of a magic formula to pay for the said puppy!

Sheila is now off to find herself in a field somewhere, sitting on a smouldering cow pat and holding hands with a group of strangers to get "grounded" and stare at the moon.

Sheila! Billy needs food this month don't be crazy now! Stop wafting lit sage around your house you're going to burn the fkn place down.

Your insurance doesn't cover stupidity just stop it!

Stop blaming the moon and some retrograde nonsense........SHEILA!!! You didn't do the work love, you were shit yesterday and you'll be shit tomorrow if you don't stop waiting for a magic pill to pop! The moon will not help you FFS!

Here's some advice for all you Sheilas out there;

1. If you are going to go self-employed - do the work and show up
2. You need to set solid foundations, a business is not the same as a BIZness that's a hobby.
3. A course staring at the moon without doing any work is not going to get you £20k months unless you are then going to sell staring at the moon courses as well
4. A vision board without work won't get you £20k months, no amount of glueing and sticking pretty pictures is going to do the work for you!
5. YOU need to do some work, Sheila!!!!
6. Buying a course and then not doing the course, will not work either!
7. If you can't grasp the need to do the work, go and get a job!
8. Stop wasting your money on courses looking for a magic formula! There isn't one!

I saw a post recently that made me double-take, they were asking for an annual UK call centre salary for one day! That's more than an audience with Richard Branson for a week and most of his fees go to the charity Virgin Unite. I could get a master's degree for half the price.

Honestly, in an unregulated market, 'coaches' are plucking these figures out of thin air with extra special bonuses added too. Apparently worth hundreds if not thousands of pounds 😵 I love the special emojis they use too;

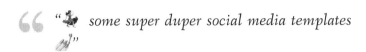 *" some super duper social media templates "*

I knocked up on Canva earlier today, and available for free to anyone with an account. Also don't miss out on this beauty,

*"the exact copy I use for my posts worth a gazillion 💰!"*

Aaaamazzzzing! If Sheila was bright enough she would realise she could go and get the exact copy from the posts the coach posts without paying thousands for it!

*"I also have for you, not to be missed an excel spreadsheet for running your own BIZness"*

You've all seen these types of posts and sponsored ads I'm sure.

You are running your business on an excel spreadsheet?

Wow, take my money!

They make up some weird titles for themselves in a completely unregulated market and sell you the dream that they can make you a millionaire when they themselves are living hand to mouth and scraping a few quid together on a Friday night for a chippy supper!

We have to turn a blind eye to the fact they have never actually qualified themselves in any way with a coaching education or credentials, real-life business experience or business acumen. It's okay though because, they used to paint gel nails in their front room, worked in Mcdonald's and made a few quid from it, they are experienced now in BIZ and know how to help you!

*'What the actual fuck!!!'* - who is buying into this nonsense??? I'll tell you who, desperate to get out of her shit life Sheila!

*'Sheila if you need a doctor call a doctor, if you need a mechanic call a mechanic, for the love of god stop seeking business advice from people who can't even run their own businesses properly never mind offer you advice on yours! ask a professional with qualifications and experience!'*

Let me tell you, anyone that uses the word BIZ to describe business is a fucking cockwomble! I cringe for them. They have probably never owned a real business a day in their entire life or at best only held junior positions in someone else's business. They've now given themselves a CEO title

(oh fucking please! of yourself and your £200 cashflow?  )

They take your money and then don't fucking show up and even worse don't deliver the goods (don't forget to read the small print), and then try to blame you for not being *'Positive and spiritual enough Sheila, it's the law of attraction, it's your own fault'*.

I can think of quite a few people like this. I've been told of many more, and these people continue to get away with this 'Emperor's New Clothes' approach to business and tarnishing a coaching industry which was previously professional and well respected. The lines are becoming blurred and something needs to be done soon to get it regulated.

The followers of these people gush, happy clap and take selfies around them like they are some kind of god or A-list celebrity. Yet they are all skint and recycling the same £10k amongst themselves and their tight-knit circle.

They create debt, depression and destruction in their path and leave you believing it's because you didn't do the work. And worst of all no one dares to say a thing for fear of being bullied about speaking up and the gushing star-struck mob lynching them.

They brag about their online success and income, wallowing in their own show of look at me, look how wonderful I am, while the people who have scraped their last pounds and dimes together to pay for this bullshit are struggling to pay their rent or buy a cooked meal.

It's hard to tell the good from the bad because so much copycatting and blatant lying on income, earnings, revenue and profit is going on as well.

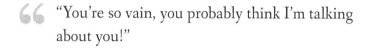 "You're so vain, you probably think I'm talking about you!"

Here's a real-life example:

Imagine a coach rocking up online selling 'high-ticket' coaching. Infiltrating everyone's social circles via friends in common, after already scamming people and leaving them high and dry on their wedding days via a failed wedding business?

Well, yes, they did, this happened.

Now here they are on Facebook pretending to have multiple 7 and 8-figure businesses that don't exist, having successes they've never had, taking people's money with a promise of writing contract proposals something they have never written before in their lives, promising to obtain you 'high ticket' leads and sales, and then nothing appears?

Bragging about buying an island, a Ferrari, and luxury leather luggage amongst other shit and it's all lies, every single word of it and all of her newfound followers fall for it hook line and sinker!!!

Why?

Well because this person had socially qualified herself by association and a few selfies, so no one doubted or questioned the lies.

The lies got bigger, '*I just sold two football clubs - wow, now I'm poolside sipping a long island tea! If you want this scammy life sign up here it's £7777 because I like 7's they are all spiritual and I'm feeling generous it's my human design code.*'

Word vomit!

The people wowed even more, and the cycle of '*take my money, take my money*' got rinsed and repeated while she's fkn laughing she's got away with it and sipping mojitos every Monday!

Her victims were left thinking it was their fault for not getting the results they expected, ashamed, they told no one, and commenced the depressing journey of paying off their debts to narrowly escape bankruptcy.

And so, the lies continued and more people got sucked in.

And when the scam unfolded and began to be told, the sob story and perfect excuse of '*my mental health made me do it'* emerged. Oh fucking, please!!! Did your mental health make your husband go along with it too?

When you see stuff like this online, don't just believe it and hand your life savings over, or max out your credit cards - have some curiosity about the posts at the very least and see if you can validate them as true, do your due diligence.

It is pretty easy to find out if an island has just been sold and how much for it took me 5 minutes on the phone with an estate agent to find out she was lying. There was no island, it was a lie and the biggest mistake she had made, it was the commencement of her downfall. Oh and meeting me for lunch, I read people and I knew she was a liar and I'm certain she knew I knew.

I remember the first time I met this 'coach' saying to a friend who knew her, *'if she's a coach and earning what she is claiming she's earning I'll eat my hat and yours!"*

I was willing to bet my year's salary on it, I knew she was lying.

Also selling a tent you don't use anymore, for a couple of hundred quid on Facebook when you are earning 8 figures sniffs of bullshit to me. 8-figure earners don't tend to sleep in tents they usually have RVs trackside or 5* Luxury suites.

I was asked recently why I don't like to sell online given all of the skills in business that I have, my answer was *'it's all nonsense, I don't want to be associated with it.'*

I've been a Business Consultant to corporates for 13 years, and have worked in corporate for 24 years now, *'hold the front page'* my work involves coaching, mentoring, and training people in business, and I don't want to tarnish my reputation by being put in the same pot as these people.

I have run businesses with turnovers in excess of £100million per annum, a few hundred staff and thousands of customers. When I support business owners it's from a place of lived experience and qualification. There is a huge difference between what you get from Tracy and her online BIZ coaching and her look-at-me photos.

Let me be 100% clear, there are some excellent business people in the online space, and I know a few of them. The problem we all have is knowing who they are and being able to spot the bad ones from the *'fake it until you make it'* chancers.

If someone is being paid to tell you to buy someone else's course (affiliate or referral marketing) ask yourself, are they recommending it because they have benefitted from it and can honestly with integrity vouch for them, or are they trying to make a few quid from selling it and have no idea if its any good or not?

Try asking people who have worked with them before but aren't recommending or affiliating - get a rounded, full-body picture, not just a paid one, especially for 'High Ticket' courses or masterminds.

The claims about making money just make me want to vomit! There's about as much class in them as a Primark paper bag!

The unregulated online business and coaching space, I score you - *'you must be fucking joking.'*

## CORPORATE PAYMENT TERMS

Corporate clients who expect you to work the month in advance and for you to then offer them 60-day payment terms because it suits their archaic invoicing process - The Jokers! *"Are you being fucking serious?"*

Tell Alison in accounts to sort her fucking shit out. You wouldn't wait for 3 months to get paid, so why do you expect contractors and consultants to? It's a big red flag and a no from me.

How about your corporate finance team starts supporting small businesses by paying upfront, or at the end of each month worked? Let's be honest being paid on time without the need for hours of payment chasing would be a miracle, we have got enough to do!

66

# Fraud is the daughter of greed.

JONATHAN GASH

## ② SHOPPING & SERVICE

## SUPERMARKETS

I STARTED my career at the age of 14 working in a cooperative hypermarket. I saw all sorts in the aisles and coming through the tills.

There are a few types of people who go shopping in supermarkets nowadays;

- The Pensioner - just for something to do
- The Efficient - I prepared a list and I'm sticking to it
- The Not Prepared - buys anything they see and thinks fuck it
- The Dawdler - hasn't got a fucking clue what they want so takes forever in every aisle.

- The Budgeter - checks the price of every item, monitoring their food budget to the exact penny.
- The Stressed Out Parent - all of the above traits except pensioner
- The Tik Toker

## Pensioners

You've had all fucking week Doris, why are you clogging up the Asda aisle on a weekend? FFS keep moving, this isn't a social gathering love, move along. I can't get to the beans because you and Elsie have blocked two bays off with the empty trolleys you are using as zimmer frames, whilst chatting because you haven't seen each other since yesterday. Doris is kindly filling Elsie in on all the gossip;

Doris - *'Bob from across the road, you know Bob, oh what's his surname now, you know Bob?'*
Elsie' - *'Is he Freda's husband?'*
Doris *'Yes god rest his soul. Yes, well he's dead! Died Tuesday, yeah shocking!'*
Elsie - *'How awful!'*
Doris -*'I think it was that new thing, you know, ooo what do they call it now? '*
Elsie - *' Was it that Chickenpox?'*
Doris - *'No love, the other one?'*
Elsie - *'Oh you mean that monkey one, don't you?*

*awful poor Freda, finding out like this he was
sleeping with monkeys, it takes all sorts you just
never know who's next door do you?'
Doris - 'Terrible, mind you he was 81 so he had a
good innings, I never thought he would've had it
in him'
Elsie - 'Well he clearly had something in him to
catch that!'*

Doris! Elsie! Just fucking move will you. FML!

## Efficient

There is a flaw in the efficient plan. A shopping ninja they are not. Long stares in the aisles while they try to find everything on their list, comparing every price tag and label and checking if buying a multi-pack is actually cheaper. Occasionally stopping to say hello to Doris and Elsie. They also love a food label and checking for those all-important calories and nuts.

## Not Prepared

This is my approach to shopping. Like a ninja, aisle by aisle just chucking anything in that catches my eye, and also remembering some of the items I buy every week, fruit, veg, milk, cheese etc. When it comes to everything else, god knows what I arrive home with. We unpack the shopping then order takeout for tea because I bought a load of fucking random shit that won't make a decent meal.

## The Dawdler

I swear to god these shoppers are just taking an hour or two to themselves while they don't have their other half and kids with them. They slowly, slowly wander around each aisle, mentally meal-prepping as they put food in their trolley. The dawdler is also the put shit back on shelves in the wrong places shopper because they have changed their minds and can't be arsed to walk back to the correct aisle to put it back.

## The Budgeter

FML try not to get caught behind one of these and a Doris or you are screwed you are going to be stuck in the aisle for the afternoon. If you see a suspected budgeter at the till, back off and choose another one because a coupon pile the height of mount Vesuvius is about to be whipped from their handbag or pocket.

## The Stressed-Out Parent

These shoppers have got a kid or two in tow in the trolley, then out the trolley, picking up all sorts of shit off the shelves and helping themselves to anything they see. Then when mum or dad tries to remove it from the trolley and put it back, the kid turns into the exorcist and goes fucking mental. Screaming the aisle down, and then all the '*oh what a shit parent they are*' looks follow, usually from Doris and Elsie who have been stood in your way for ten fkn minutes.

## The Tik Toker

Nowadays it's not uncommon to turn the corner in an aisle and see someone dancing in front of the cornflakes and coco pops. Their phones are propped up by a multipack of Kellogg's and off they go.

For anyone who isn't on TikTok this behaviour just looks mental. They observe and wonder if they should fetch security because it's all going off in aisle 6 and no one can access the cereal.

Supermarket shopping and your weird and wonderful shoppers I am scoring you the honour of '*what the actual fuck*' is it any wonder so many of us have swapped to Morrisons via amazon!

# SHOPPING TROLLEYS

There are trolleys that annoy me because lazy people haven't bothered taking them back to the trolley park and just left them rolling around the carpark smashing into my car.

You go to turn into a car parking space and realise as you have committed to turn in some lazy git has left their trolley there *'oh for fucks sake!'* so annoying!

Then there's the dodgy trolley with the wonky wheel and the squeak. The trolley is full of wet till receipts and empty wet carrier bags! I'm not a fan of supermarket trolleys at all.

*'FML I always get the wonky wheel!'*

## A FEW ITEMS

Those people who have a trolley bursting at the seams, and all you have is a pint of milk, which is going to take 30 seconds to pay for. They look at you, smile and carry on loading the conveyor belt with their shopping.

They are under no obligation whatsoever to say *'oh is that all you have, here, you go ahead and go first'* and guess what? these 'knob jockeys', they fkn don't either! RUDE!

## FOOD & PRODUCT LABELS

Which bright spark invented food and product labelling?

Ready Salted Peanuts - may contain nuts, fuck off no, really!?! I would never have guessed a bag of peanuts contained nuts. Are we really that bloody stupid nowadays we can't grasp the simple things in life.

––––––––

Like warning labels on bleach - don't drink it, mmm tasty, dam there goes my Friday night tipple. Who in their right fucking mind wants to drink bleach FFS. These labels are clearly there for the morons in society. Let me tell you if they are that fucking stupid to be drinking bleach we should perhaps let them crack on!

––––––––

Suppositories insert into your back passage. DO NOT SWALLOW. I'm going to assume you either know you are constipated or you know you have piles. The remedy to which you have recently purchased the said suppositories for relief of the condition.

66 *"Why the fuck would you swallow them?"*

If you are dumb enough to think swallowing a suppository is going to fix your piles there is something seriously wrong with you!

––––––––

The grotesque imagery placed on cigarette packets nowadays, perhaps if they tried just showing how much tax was added per pack and the cost of them it would gain better results. Even better positive messaging on what they could save and what they could have if they gave up. Does this imagery even work?

What happened to choice? If they want to smoke let them, the bloody government has caused more deaths and health issues with lockdowns and covid jabs than smoking ever will.

———

Calorie information on packets and tins requires you to have a dart player's ability to compute numbers. They never actually tell you how many calories are in your bag, do they? A 30g bag of crisps usually tells you the 100g value and expects you to do the math. Not helpful at all!

———

Best before and use-by dates just cause food waste and more arguments in our house than I care to mention! My husband religiously throws stuff away because of these dates it drives me mad! I go to grab the piccalilli out of the fridge for my cheese sandwich and it's not there because it's been open for 6 weeks so he's binned it - fuming!!!

Food labels and your useless advice and nonsense calorie counting, you score a *'you must be fucking joking me.'* you are clearly keeping some knob jockey in a job.

## TIPS

A voluntary tip/service charge, which is already added to your bill? *'you must be fucking joking.'*

Your service was really shit, and now you expect me to tip you for it? Jog on. There's nothing voluntary about a tip that's added without consent, and then making the customer feel awkward asking you to remove it.

I have asked for it to be removed on several occasions, and then confronted on why,

*'Well, I tip great service or even good, but yours was rubbish, the food was cold, you took over an hour to bring us our food, and then you got our drinks orders wrong three fucking times, we asked for the bill forty minutes ago and told you we needed to leave, you've been useless all night and now you want me to reward you?'* - this actually happened in a Jamie Oliver restaurant in London after a night at the theatre.

Pre-added tips you are getting scored - *'you can fuck right off!'*

## INSURANCE AT THE TILL

Going into an electronics store and the cashier is immediately trying to sell you extra insurance. The washing machine you are about to purchase, it's got a 3-year warranty with it, and now the cashier is putting you off buying it because it needs some extra warranty because it's that shit it's going to break down on you next week and parts and labour aren't included in the warranty it has!

No thanks, I'll take my chances!

Point of sale insurance policies - *'What in the glorious fuck are you talking about?!?'*

## CLOTHES SIZES

According to Next, I'm a size 16, If I shop in George at Asda I'm a size 12/14. If I go into any garden centre, they have given up on the bullshit of sizing and have gone for a one-size-fits-all approach!

I quite like it, elasticated waist trousers which grow, expand and shrink with me and my menopausal body. If I go for a curry they expand, I go for a 💩 they shrink back down, it's great.

I guess what I'm trying to say is, from one store to the next sizes are never accurate and trying to measure yourself in terms of look and feel good should not be done by jeans sizes. Don't beat yourself up because you may need a size up in one store versus the other. Wear what is comfy and makes you feel good.

Cloth sizing I award you the score of - *'what the actual fuck'*


## DO YOU WANT A BAG?

Do I want a bag? *'No, Susan, I'm going to carry all seventy-three items in my arms and hope I don't drop something on the way to my car. I would be so annoyed if one of my granny smiths went rolling down the carpark, but fuck it I'm feeling all adventurous today so I will pass on the 5p bag'* - said no one EVER!!!!

Of course, I want a fkn bag Susan!! If you can't see me holding a bag for life with a trolley full of shopping on the belt, then you are asking the most ridiculous of questions.

Do I want a bag for my week's shopping? I award you *'Are you being fucking serious?'*


## SECURITY TAGS

This actually cracks me up every time I think about it.

This is a true story. My mum, in her 70's, bought herself a new winter coat, from Roman Originals. On purchasing said coat she left the store and the security alarms went off, bleeping really loud at the doors. She was obviously embarrassed and showed the woman her receipt and checked her bag. She had her walk in and out a few times and they were satisfied she had actually paid for the coat and had nothing else on her person.

Mum went uptown in the new coat the next day and in every store, she walked into or out of, the security alarms went off. My mum was getting really cheesed off by being stopped and checked everywhere she went. Having to show she had either got nothing on her or the receipt for goods if she had bought something. It was beyond embarrassing. This went on for a few weeks every time she went out, in every shop she went into.

As soon as the alarms went off on entering a store she would say *'I've not even come in yet!'* Honestly, she was fuming.

On a shopping trip with her sister a couple of weeks later, it had started to rain so mum popped the hood up on the coat and continued to wander around town until my aunty saw the back of her head and the hood proudly displaying a grey security tag for all to see.

My aunty was laughing her head off and my mum was going mad not knowing why she was laughing. She had been walking around town for at least three weeks in and out of shops putting her hood up when she was outside for all except her to see this bloody tag on the hood. No one in the store could see it as she put the hood down to enter the store.

Security tags left on newly purchased clothes, especially your new holiday clothes and you don't notice until the night before you fly or even worse when you get there. I'm awarding you a '*oh just fuck off*'.


# DFS

When you wander into DFS to sofa surf and three sales staff ask you what you're looking for today, but you're really only just browsing.

Incoming, big cheesy grin Brandon, here he is, fucking grinning ear to ear because he's about to nail your arse to that corner suite and dick you for three grand on a buy now pay next week sale!

It's the longest sale in history, who is buying into the nonsense? You aren't getting a sale item or a bargain at all, this is ridiculous taking the piss out of the public marketing and pricing fuckery!

'*Hello my name is Brandon, is there anything I can help you with today?*'

What my head is thinking is, "*oh just fuck off Brandon, give me a fucking chance to look FFS, I only came in here because it's raining and there's fuck all else to do at the weekend!*".

What comes out of my mouth is "*No thank you!*" followed by a grin filled with more cheese than a Burger King flame grilled whopper! I am now uncomfortable browsing so quickly scan the store and leave. If Brandon had just left me alone, I would probably have bought a sofa, but no he had to go and spoil it didn't he???

Sales assistants who pounce on you as soon as you walk into a store '*just fuck off.*'

## CUSTOMER SERVICE

I have championed customer experience in business for a very long time. I specialise in developing world-class customer journeys.

However, this phrase really does get my backup!

 "The customer is always right!"

No, the customer is most definitely sometimes a twat.

Some people just love to complain and try to see what they can get for free. There are even online forums telling you how to get companies to give you compensation for making the slightest of expressions of dissatisfaction.

I really do feel sorry for the contact centre workers of brands that get their service so wrong. The abuse they put up with on low incomes is just not fair.

For god's sake folks, think before you start screaming down the phone at them, they are probably on national minimum wage and have no other choice than working there to put food on the table. You are taking your frustrations out on the wrong employee, it's those at the top, those in charge who are to blame.

The service industry could do better, so much better. I know I've been banging on about service improvement for years now.

Energy Suppliers, Banks, Broadband providers, Mobile phone providers, and Insurance companies to name a few.

Those IVR systems which ask you to press 1, then press 4, then press 6 then cut you off after they didn't answer for 30-minutes, are just shocking.

The gate swings in both directions, if you are a consumer please don't abuse customer service staff when you need to complain. And customer service staff please try to be a little more understanding and have less of a condescending attitude.

Customers and customer service, *'fuckity fuck fuck!'*

## DOCTORS RECEPTIONISTS

I'm going to stick doctor's surgeries under customer service because as patients we are also customers of that practice.

Here I go off on my rant and I think I will be joined by every man, woman and child in the sheer frustration of an encounter with KAREN 'The Receptionist'!

Who appointed these people to be the gatekeepers, diagnostic consultants and god FFS! Doctors surgeries your customer service is quite possibly the worst I have ever known. There is no excuse for rudeness and attitude.

I swear to god, this industry needs my F*CK! toolkit to help it to get its fkn act together! Getting an appointment with a doctor prior to covid-19 was a nightmare now it's nigh on impossible.

I don't care what industry you are in, you need clients, consumers, and customers to drive revenue into your business to pay your wages. Therefore you should be showing a degree of customer care.

*"I'm not asking for bells and whistles here Karen, I'm asking for a fkn appointment. No, no Karen I don't want to phone up every morning at 8am to be told there are no appointments left, fuck-off!!!! Two weeks, two fucking weeks are you fucking joking I will either be dead, in the hospital or healed by then, are you fucking joking???"*

It would appear the doctor's surgeries are now a law unto themselves and have decided patients are no longer worth seeing, just let Karen the receptionist from the bowels of hell speak to them.

I am awarding doctors and their rude receptionists *'Are you being fucking serious?'*

**"We are so conformist; nobody is thinking. We are all sucking up stuff; we have been trained to be consumers, and we are all consuming far too much.**

VIVIENNE-WESTWOOD

# PEOPLE

## GRAMMAR AND SPELLING POLICE

I THOUGHT I'd get three chapters in before I hit you with this one. If you have spotted mistakes in the book, great I'm human!

They're, There, Their, Your, You're and many others, marvellous, did it prevent you from understanding what I have written? I doubt it!

Grammar and spelling police online who point these things out publicly to try and get themselves a gold star and make the person who made the error look like an idiot, you are a cockwomble!

*'Just fuck off'* - Did I spell that right?

## PEOPLE WATCHING

Do you ever just sit and people-watch? I love observing people. On the beach, at train stations, at airports, in the supermarket (I bet Doris and Elsie are still in aisle 5), and at restaurants. We are all so busy, aren't we? Except for the dawdler (more on the dawdler below we also met them whilst shopping).

I have running commentary going on in my head, especially at the airport;

*'aww bless him, I bet his wife dressed him, look at him in his new shorts, shirt, bright white sneakers, I bet his entire suitcase is full of brand new colour co-ordinated outfits neatly ironed and folded.'*

*'OMG did you not look at yourself before you left the house? good grief someone needs to tell her those leggings have gone see-through and we can see her pink thong and front bush.'*

*'poor woman, all those kids and her husband is acting like a right waste of space he's not helping at all.'*

*'oh god sliders and socks pulled halfway up your calf - not a good look who invents these trends you look ridiculous.'*

*'Jesus sandals and socks, oh my god haha people actually still wear them it's not just my husband oh dear'*

'There's no way they are going to let you on that plane, you've drunk too much, you idiot!'

'Jesus love, did you come straight from the night club, wow, did you forget your skirt?'

'I bet he's having an affair, business trip my arse, your banging someone on the side deffo'

'one, two, three, four....seven, seven bloody wheelchairs queueing for my flight. How do these people get off if we crash are they going to be in everyone's way?'

People Watching - 'You are fucking glorious I love you!'

## TOURISTS

Fuck my life, I could swing for tourists, especially in London. You can't walk the pavement in London without a random tourist stopping dead in the centre of the pavement to take a photo.

You have to dig your heels in and put on your brakes to avoid chucking your Cafe Nero down the back of their neck. Who in their right mind without warning or checking, just stops dead on the pavement where hundreds of other people are busily going about their day? I don't like London much for this reason. It is full of tourists!

London is the only city I know where you cross the road with at least 40 plus other people at a time.

*'It's Fkn mental!'*

———

Tourists abroad, the ones who wander into restaurants and supermarkets with no top on or just in their beachwear. They wouldn't do it at home so why do it on holiday?

*'No one wants to sit eating their lunch looking at your beer belly Fred. FFS cover your hairy back up it's minging you're putting me off my lasagna.'*

———

Tourists on the flight to get there! FML.

TripAdvisor actually surveyed 9000 people to find out what annoyed them about tourists and travelling the most;

**Top travel annoyances**

1. **Children kicking your seat back** - definitely my number 1 pet hate and the reason I always book a seat in front of the extra legroom seats or in front of an emergency exit on the wing, so small kids can't sit in the seats behind me!!

2. **Rude seat recliners** - This boils my piss!

3. **Loud mobile phone conversations** - Cringe!

4. **Passengers taking too long to stow overhead baggage** - FFS is Doris your nan?

5. **People getting up before the seatbelt sign is off** - they are the same fukwits who queue an hour and half before the plane takes off.

6. **Armrest hogs;** - This boils my piss too!

7. **Passengers consuming smelly food** - Nah not so bothered, unless I'm sat next to them and they are eating beef monster munch and stink of BO! Gag

8. **Travellers blocking moving walkways** - this also boils my piss, sit the fuck down!

9. **'Shoulder surfers' reading over your shoulder** - Rude!

10. **People wandering in front of airport service carts** - fuck off out the way you moron, I need a drink because of all of this list!

Tourists, I'm awarding you the honour of *'what the actual fuck'*

## SMOKERS

My only bug bare with people who smoke is this, getting your fags out after a meal in a restaurant (not in the UK this is in holiday destinations). Just because you can and the laws are different abroad, doesn't mean you should! Not where other people are still eating and drinking. It's disgusting and damn right rude!

Smokers who smoke where people are eating - *'what the fuck you are you doing you, dirty inconsiderate bastards.'*

## PEOPLE WHO BELCH AND FART

We all do it and if you say you don't you are lying even the Queen did it!

I honestly don't understand how though, some people can just parade around without a care in the world dropping stink and noise bombs in front of their other half or friends. Like what is going on in their minds?

I've had a fkn bellyache for 14 years holding them in around my husband! I have the fussiest of toilet habits, I struggle to use public toilets even to wee, let alone to drop my weekly shop off.

*'Listen Linda in cubicle 3, I know you're taking a shit, no amount of coughing is going to disguise the noise or stench!*

*Also if you pull any more bog roll off you are going to cause a blockage.'*

The lethal coffee shit in a morning, with the walk of butt-clenching, farting shame and sweat beads running down your forehead in case you don't get there on time and actually shit yourself.

And then there are those couples who fart and hold their partner's head under the covers in bed! I would deck them!

Then there's the older generation of farters who just get up out of a chair and fart their way to the kettle to make a brew. They casually ignore the fact it's happening, whilst the grandkids are literally fucking pissing themselves laughing!

I might be a tad jealous of you people if I'm totally honest! A life where you can fart and go to the loo anytime and place sounds fucking marvellous!

## PEOPLE WHO LITTER

See above smokers! Stop throwing your fag butts everywhere!

People driving who throw things out of their car windows into hedgerows, WTF is wrong with you!

People who litter you are the '*Prick's'* of society!

## PEOPLE WALKING DEAD SLOW - THE DAWDLER

OMG people who just shuffle along in life, on the pavements, in the park, in the supermarkets and shops and you just can't get past them because they are just dawdling along without a care in the world, blocking the main walkways.

These people are just so chilled out they are practically horizontal. Don't they have something to be doing? Do they not have any goals they are striving to achieve? They are just dead slow dawdling people. They always seem to be obstructing my path wherever I am going.

You are rushing to your train platform or airport gate and they are there in the fucking way. I'm busy and literally sprinting about the place to get all my shit done, I have places I need to be, and a damn sight quicker than the dawdler. I have goals to achieve, things to do, and money to earn....come on hurry up!

The Dawdler you are getting the honour of '*fucking speed up or move you cockwomble'*.

## PEOPLE WHO DON'T KNOW WHICH SIDE OF THE PAVEMENT TO WALK ON.

It's not obvious to most people but there is a fkn system that keeps us all moving along if we all use it! You need to keep right FFS! That way whilst you are fkn dawdling along, people like me who are speeding through life can overtake you on the opposite side.

*'Get out of the way FFS!'*

## PEOPLE ON TRAVALATORS WHO ARE JUST STANDING THERE!

Connected hotels in Las Vegas, airports, and ports, all have them. But there's always that person that instead of walking on the travelator and taking advantage of the speed it gives you to get there quicker. They just stand on it like a lazy bastard, or as if their legs are broken!

*'What in gods name is wrong with you!? fucking move!'*

## PEOPLE ON ESCALATORS

London underground fukwits, stop standing two abreast on the escalators. Stand to the fucking right so other people who aren't the dawdlers of society can get past you and get to work. We aren't all tourists in London some people need to be places to earn a living.

*'Move out of the goddamn way!!!'*

## PEOPLE WHO MUMBLE

What was that you said? You're fucking mumbling again Sheila I can't hear you or tell a word you are saying!

Speak up Sheila, lift your head up and project your voice for fucks sake! Stop fkn mumbling, how are we expected to have a conversation if I have to keep asking you to repeat yourself? God give me strength with mumblers!

*'What in the glorious fuck are you saying?!?'*

## PEOPLE WHO QUEUE

We love a good queue in the UK, don't we?

Well, I fucking don't! I think queuing is a waste of life and energy. I see all the tourists dying to get on the plane and pushing and shoving to be first in the priority boarding or first in the not priority but I want to be first on the plane anyway queue.

I just look at them all and think you bunch of morons get a grip you are all going on the same plane, does it really matter who gets on first! Even with priority boarding, I wait until last to get on, I only buy it so I can take hand luggage on and reserve the seat I want.

What the actual fuck was that queue for the Queen lying in state all about? Seriously who in their right mind wants to stand in a queue for 24 hours or more to have a 3-second walk-by of a coffin?

All credit to you if you queued and did this you've got more queuing stamina than I'll ever have and you probably loved it, I know many who did. It's a no from me though.

The Queens Queue - *'WTF I'm actually applauding your sheer brilliance and utter madness.'*

The queue for the next sale is something else as well, there are people who actually go in the middle of the night and camp out on the doorstep waiting for the store to open. WTF is wrong with you people, get a grip!

The queue to be first in for a concert, and they camp on the streets outside venues for days, like literally days on end to be first in. If I am ever seen queuing like this, please know I am probably being held against my will so come and rescue me!

The fkn queue for a PS5 at Christmas, my god!

*'Wow!'*

## GROUPS OF LOUD PEOPLE

Why? Why are you being so damn loud! Keep your volume down and stop acting like an entitled prick to the waiters or waitresses and having no regard for anyone else around you!

Are you like this sober? Oh shit, you are sober, wow you're just a C U Next Tuesday!

*'Be fucking quiet, stop shouting, sit down and stop standing on the chairs and tables!'*

# ENTITLED CLIENTS

When a client buys a *'done for you'* service from you and they turn into a fucking diva and for £30 they expect the crown jewels! Jesus Christ some people really piss me off. I mutter oh just fuck off far too often.

Clients who ask for a bespoke written proposal and a presentation which takes you hours to complete and then say *'can you do it cheaper, will you reduce your day rate'*. So you agree to a reduction and scaling back of certain items. They sign the contract but then they expect and want the titanium-plated version of your proposal they originally read before they cut it back to a lower price. *'Oh just fuck off!'*

You wouldn't work for less don't expect me to! Tosspots!

I'm not going to go into any details, other than to say just because you didn't read your contract before signing it does not mean it's not valid. Read your contract and know what you bought, and what you signed up for, stop taking the piss and expecting more than you paid for.

## WHEN YOUR CLIENT ASKS

## IF YOU CAN DO IT CHEAPER

## PEOPLE WITH LARGE SOCIAL AUDIENCES ONLINE

When a coach or 'influencer' asks you to support them with their launch and come and train their large audience in your area of expertise so they can sell them a 'course or mastermind'.

Then they drop the bomb that they expect you to do it for free, to give up your time because they have got a large audience who you will be exposed to. They tell you to drop your pricing pants so low that your piles are visible!

There are also clear rules *'you cannot sell to my audience'*, I'm sorry what? Please explain why I need to come and train my course for free and can't sell a thing to your audience how exactly am I benefitting from that?

Apparently, this will be good for your BIZness!

They talk about professional boundaries but have none of their own.

*'Oh just fuck off you freeloader, you need boundary and entitlement coaching! Even the UK government have rules about the national minimum wage. Sheila needs paying stop being a twat!'*

## SPLITTING THE BILL

People who say, yeah, let's just split the bill, when they've ordered a bottle of champagne, a starter, a main and pudding with four gin and tonics, a Brandy and a double espresso shot to finish the night off. Meanwhile, you had Lasagna and chips with a diet coke.

And they now declare we are splitting the bill!! WTF!!! Why should I pay for your meal? Are you actually fucking joking? Pay for your own meal you entitled knob jockey!

Fair enough if we've all had roughly the same split it, who's arguing over loose change? But there's a stark difference between my £9.99 main and your lavish £163 meal.

*'I'm not your top-up account! Off you fucking trot you freeloader!'*

## NOISY EATERS

OMG noisy eaters are just the worst!

Also, people who chew with their mouths open, and have their tonsils on show whilst eating a meal. Shut your mouth, you're making me gag! WTF is wrong with you is your jaw misaligned when you chew or something?

And while we are here, when you get to the bottom of that drink with your straw, there is just no fucking need to keep sucking and making that noise. What are you like five or something??

*'For fucks sake! stop it!'*

## WHEN ANYONE KNOCKS ON MY DOOR

I can't tell you how annoyed I feel. When random people knock on my door unexpectedly trying to sell me shit. Or when people just turn up out of the blue and you were trying to watch a movie or take a nap or were just about to get it on with your other half and now they've spoiled the moment!!! They are banging on the door expecting a chat and a brew!

I particularly despise Jehovah's Witnesses knocking on my door and trying to pass me a magazine all about Jesus – oh just FUCK OFF!!

I welcome anyone to my home, just tell me you are coming first so I can mentally prepare myself! I have to gear up for this stuff.

## WHEN SOMEONE ON FACEBOOK SAYS SOMETHING OBSCURE FOR ATTENTION

This really gets my back up and I end up thinking I hope your day gets worse Carol you C*NT!

People are commenting on your post and you are replying, I've DM'd you hun! Oh just fuck off you attention-seeking twat!

## WHEN RICH PEOPLE ASK YOU TO DONATE MONEY

What the fuck are you giving?

If all the wealthy people put their money to work, world hunger would end! They could stop poverty today but choose not to, instead they ask us to pay, while they are off flying into space for ten minutes!

*'Are you fucking kidding me?'*

## PEOPLE FACEBOOK SUGGESTS YOU ADD AS A FRIEND

All I'm saying is there's a reason you aren't on my friend list already! Wendy from school who you haven't seen in forty years, and Dave from the garage who put new tyres on the car three years ago, his mobile number happens to be in your phone and that's the only reason Facebook thinks its a good idea!

Your ex who's created a new profile because they are trying to stalk you via friends in common. No thank you!

*You must be fucking joking!*

## SMELLY PEOPLE

OMFG have you ever smelt that person, somewhere in public, in a store, on a train, or bus and they just FKN stink like stale piss. Like they pissed themselves two weeks ago and haven't washed, cleaned their clothes or showered in months! The stench makes your eyes sting.

How do they not know how bad they smell?

Some genuinely clean people stink sour because they didn't dry their clothes properly and for some strange reason haven't seemed to realise they stink!

Then there are people with really bad BO, omg get a wash and buy some decent deodorant for god's sake.

Have you ever been in a meeting and someone has done the make myself look bigger hands behind their head pose, peacocking and two great big sweaty armpit stains appear, it has me gagging. Put your bloody arms down for god's sake it looks awful. If you have this issue you can actually buy pads for your armpits (it's actually a thing, it clearly annoyed me that much I researched it for someone I worked with!) like a pant liner but for armpits and shirts.

## PEOPLE ON THEIR PHONES IN A RESTAURANT

I have eaten out in restaurants far too many times and sadly witnessed families and couples ignoring each other in favour of scrolling on their phones.

WHY??? WTF is wrong with you, you are with your family or loved ones get off your fkn phone and talk to one another, one day they will be gone, what then?

I am awarding you the honour of '*cockwomble!*'

## PEOPLE WHO TALK IN CINEMAS

For those of you that know me, you will know this absolutely makes me lose my absolute shit! I've paid to go and watch a movie, and should be able to hear the damn thing!

I have on more than one occasion told the people around me to '*shut the fuck up or get out.*'

I honestly just think people who talk through films are so bloody inconsiderate and rude, I don't much care about going to the cinema for this reason as one of these days I will end up lamping someone.

## PEOPLE WHO ARE NOISY IN THE QUIET CAB OF A TRAIN

This particular person wasn't vocally noisy, she was busy tapping away on her laptop like it was a drum kit, with the longest fucking false nails you have ever seen. Click, Click, Click, Click - oh just fuck off! Type fucking quieter you twat it's the most irritating noise in the world!!!

## PEOPLE WHO DON'T RSVP

Someone has been kind enough to send you an invite, include you, and remember you. They have literally gone out of their way to send you a card or digital invitation to something, like their birthday or engagement party and you can't even be arsed to RSVP them to let them know you are going or not.

*'Are you fucking joking?'* Why! Why do you find that so hard you knob jockey?

## LATE PEOPLE OR NO SHOWS

Do you know something that gets me really, really riled up? It is people who book meetings with me and then don't bother turning up. Like, why is my time not as important as their time? And then when I log off the call after waiting for 10 minutes (which I think is more than generous of me, sitting there twiddling my thumbs waiting) and they come on the call 15 minutes later wondering where I am. Like it's my fkn problem that they were late.

You failed to communicate you were running late, I've already left, love. You didn't turn up. You didn't respect my time. *'Fuck off you Cockwomble.'*

*'I was actually ten minutes late to a zoom call the other day, what a knob! I couldn't get off my other call to even explain I was running late. It annoys me when I do it to other people so you can imagine how I feel when its done to me'*

## PEOPLE WHO SAY 'CAN I GET'

This drives me mad. There is no excuse for being rude to anyone who is serving you food and drink. There is a really simple phrase, it's called 'May I please have...." or "Please may I have" not "Can I get" - Can you get? Yes, you can get, you can get the hell out of here! Manners cost nothing, use them.

'*Stop treating service industry staff like third-rate citizens they are not! Don't be a dick!*'

## HOLDING THE DOOR

You are fucking welcome Malcolm! No don't mind me I'll fucking stand here holding the door for you, while you let it go in the face of Sheila and her brood of kids trying to get through the door behind you.

'*How fkn rude!*'

## PEOPLE WHO SHAKE AND TAP THEIR FEET

My husband does this on the sofa at night, I don't even think he knows he does it so much and causes the sofa to shake and rock. It winds me up so bad.

'*Sit fucking still or fuck off on another chair!*'

## WHISTLERS

'*Is there something fucking wrong with you? You jovial tosspots shut the fuck up!*' Whistling! Who wants to listen to that row while walking around Asda or on a train?

## HEADPHONES

Are you deaf or just plain ignorant? If you are on public transport, let's say a train or plane, and you have your gangster rap shit on that loud three rows behind us can hear it, then you are an ignorant arsehole!

Have you any idea how damaging listening to music that loud is for your eardrums? Listen to me, I now sound like your fkn nan!

*'Turn your music down you tosspot!'*

## PANTS ON SHOW

Lads for fucks sake pull your fucking jeans up! What do you look like? I'll tell you what, a sack of shit that's what. No one needs to see your undercrackers on show and skid marks from 3-day-old boxers. Who invents these ridiculous trends, this one and fkn jeans on backwards you look like mummy didn't dress you today!

**66**

# Don't confuse my personality with my attitude. My personality is who I am and my attitude depends on who you are

ANONYMOUS

# 4

# TELEVISION, MOVIES AND MAINSTREAM MEDIA

## TV LICENSING

JUST FUCK OFF! - you cockwombles!

The fucking BBC are you having a laugh? They now want you to have a licence for Amazon Prime and Youtube!

So let me get this straight, you want me to get a TV licence to watch content my mate creates that's already full of adverts and ad-free for a paid membership? You had nothing to do with it, it cost you fuck all but you think I owe you something? I don't think so.

The TV licence is outdated and needs closing down, a bit like the government, it's run its course and needs rethinking! We don't have 3 channels anymore you've lost your monopoly and to be quite frank I'd rather watch paint dry than BBC rubbish!

TV Licensing for just being an absolute rip-off merchant alone gets you the - "C U Next Tuesday" award.

## IT'S TIME TO WATCH A MOVIE

The whole family has settled down to watch a brand new film or it's just you and your friend, husband, wife or partner. It is inevitable two things are now going to happen.

One of you is going to say *'ooo which film have I seen him/her in before?'* and then miss the next fifteen minutes of the film looking up the cast name to find out what other films it could be you've seen them in before.

Then they then pipe up, *'who's she, why is she going there, what's that for, and the best one 'does he/she die?'*

News flash!!! I haven't seen the fucking film before either I have no idea what happens, just watch the bloody film.

Watching movies with someone I award you - *'shut the fuck up and watch it FFS!'*

## TITANIC

*'Rose, budge up you selfish cow, FFS Jack didn't need to die!'*

Were you suffering from body dysmorphia or something, that door was plenty big enough for the two of you.

*'Fucking hell Rose, what were you thinking?'*

## LORD OF THE RINGS

Sorry to any of you LOTR fans reading this. By the end of the first film and he still had that fucking ring, I was getting ready to push him into that volcano myself! 2 hours 58 minutes of my life I'll never get back.

LOTR you are getting a *'What the actual fuck!'*

I haven't watched any of the others, although my best mate loves them. The first one was enough for me.

## BATSHIT CRAZY DALLAS

Sorry if you weren't around in the 80s, I'm probably going to lose you for a few minutes while I indulge myself in memories of this WTF just happened TV show. It aired on a Friday evening sometimes at 9pm sometimes at 10pm, the great thing was I got to stay up late it was a real treat!

The two main storylines for me were;

1. Who shot JR
2. Bobby Ewing in the Shower

First up Who shot JR, it was 1980 I was 9 years old and this storyline literally gripped the nation, it became mainstream news and had the bookies going crazy. Pretty much everyone on the show was a suspect. It generated millions of dollars in revenue just from 'Who shot JR' merchandise, it was a piece of television marketing genius, where the BBC actually earned their licensing fee.

It was one of the best 'who done it', pieces of tv history I've ever seen. It took the show 8 months to reveal who it was. An ex-sister-in-law and former mistress. This literally left you thinking WTF I would never have guessed it was her. I desperately wanted it to be his wife Sue Ellen or Cliff Barnes his arch-rival.

Second up Bobby Ewing in the shower. Allow me to set the scene for the biggest piece of TV bullshit you have ever witnessed in your entire life, in stark contrast to the who shot JR script, this was car crash viewing and laughable.

The Associated Press called it the "most famous shower scene since Psycho."

In season eight of Dallas in 1985 Bobby Ewing was killed off. It was a dramatic exit as he was ploughed over by a speeding vehicle. Season nine aired and Bobby Ewing was no longer in the show, he was dead.

So imagine everyone's reaction at the end of season nine, when his wife wakes up to the sound of a running shower and declares she's just had a really bad dream. Bobby Ewing her dead husband is in the shower soaping himself up and casually appears from behind the shower screen. Rendering the whole of season nine null and void. As viewers we had to try and forget a whole season had happened, it was all a bad dream. Disastrous TV, it lost all credibility after then, the move was seen as a desperate attempt to recover viewing figures.

Dallas I am awarding you the honour of *'What in the glorious fuck were you thinking?'*

## MAINSTREAM MEDIA

 "He who has the most money controlleth the narrative!"

The media is not run by true journalists anymore it is run by elitists with a narrative and an agenda. Journalists have become lazy, they regurgitate a narrative passed to them and hardly bother investigating if what they are regurgitating is satisfactorily true to the best of their knowledge and factual or not.

Fact-checkers are also spreading lies as well, as I've said before most people are too lazy to research so they trust the mainstream media to tell the truth and they believe what they see, hear and read.

I don't trust any of it anymore it's all fkn bullshit, bent truths and lies! Donald Trump wasn't wrong calling out all the 'Fake News', he was spot on, a president gone rogue, he had to go, he didn't fit the establishment. Perhaps Elon Musk is going to allow him back on Twitter?

I'm going to say a few words here which started my descent to researching my own truths several years ago 'Millie Dowler' and 'Hillsborough'.

Have you noticed all the fact-checked posts which come up on social media warning you about something especially covid-19. (I do come to that later in chapter 9)

They have all the technology to spot a racist post yet they continue to allow them to get through? The algorithms could easily stamp it out on their platforms but they don't, funny that? The algorithms could easily prevent a lot of things but it chooses not to, the technology is there, yet still, moving along there is nothing to see here!

Mainstream media and lazy journalists I award you the honour of *'What in the glorious fuck are you talking about?!?'*

## ADVERTS

Far too many of them, everything is over-commercialised to within an inch of its existence! The BBC still want you to pay for a TV licence! I know I started with TV licensing but here I am again on my soap box.

I have mixed feelings for adverts, I don't mind them so much, whereas my husband fkn hates them to the point we don't watch live TV anymore, he gets so irate at adverts.

I actually love their creativity, some of them are actually better than the shows on TV.

I'm fairly neutral on adverts, it's a topic that made it into the book so maybe they do piss me off sometimes, or perhaps it's my husband's reaction to them that pisses me off.

So I'm going to award my husband the honour of '*what a load of old bollocks, shut the fuck up moaning!*'

## STAR WARS VERSUS HARRY POTTER

" "Harry Potter is just Star Wars with sucky lightsabers"

— AARON WOODALL, COMEDIAN

I absolutely adore both of these film franchises. I've loved Star Wars since childhood. Obviously being a mum of three, Harry Potter was a huge franchise in our house too as they were growing up. So were Twilight and 50 Shades of Grey, I must stress I didn't force my three young kids to watch 50 Shades FFS, that was for my viewing pleasure only, I'd go into his red room any day of the week! Mmmmm where was I, I drifted off there to somewhere else.

Oh Star Wars and Harry Potter!

I have to agree with Aaron on this, the similarities in the story outline are really hard to ignore.

It really does appear as though JK Rowling has ripped off Star Wars! No, seriously, go and check it out for yourself. You don't need to search far to find the evidence!

J K - *'Are you fucking kidding me?'*

———

I watch so little TV nowadays that I'm finding it hard to even think WTF to write here. Oh no hang on a minute, I have one more thing to say, **Uhtred of Bebbanburg!**

What the FUCK....If he isn't making your fanny flutter check your pulse! As you were ladies, as you were! Thank you to my best friend Abigail, I'm paying this forward.

**There are two things you never turn down: sex and appearing on television.**

GORE VIDAL

## 5

## DRIVING

## HGVS ON MOTORWAYS

HAVE you ever been driving on a motorway and you've decided it was time to indicate, pull out into the centre lane to overtake the HGV in front of you?

Ok, so you now know the scenario we are in!

Right as you are alongside them they start indicating and leave you in a blind panic wondering if they actually know you are there alongside them or if are you in a blind spot about to be trashed over into the fast lane and probably cause a pileup?

I go absolutely mental at this point, *'are you fucking kidding me, are you blind what the fuck are you doing, why not fucking wait until I've passed you!!! Just fuck-off!!'*

Just me?

Also on the topic of motorways, if that's you Janice in your fucking BMW hogging the middle lane on the M6 all the way to Preston, you are a C U Next Tuesday, #justsaying.

## CYCLISTS

London cyclists - mad as fucking hatters, crazy bastards have you seen how busy London is? Don't ever mess with a London cyclist they have balls of steel!

Country road cyclists - lycra wankers I like to call them, hogging up the middle of the road so you can't get past them during a national speed limit zone. Sometimes two or three a breast! Get out of the way you morons!

In the town on the way to work cyclists, you know the ones, with cycle clips around their ankles looking like their nan dresses them. They remind me of Mr Bean. Then they turn up at the office dripping with fkn sweat and getting smellier as the day goes on because these morons don't shower when they arrive, they've cycled in wearing their suits! They then sit in meetings peacocking to cool down with their sweaty armpits on show for all to see.

Recumbent bikes! WTAF! What are these all about, the rider is laid practically horizontal staring up at the sky, while the traffic around them tries to navigate getting past them not knowing if they even know they share the road space with other vehicles. Most of them have a long flag sticking up out of the back of them. I honestly can't see the point in them.

Cyclists you belong somewhere else just not on the main roads, especially roads where I'm driving. I award you a strong *'Fuck my actual life!'* for all the frustrating times I've been stuck behind you!

## SPEED LIMITS

OMG 30mph feels so slow on a country road, why are they changing all the speed limits to make us all go even slower? The cars are getting faster, while the speed limits are restricted all around us.

We may as well go back to the horse and cart if the snowflakes reduce them anymore. Everyone has these curtailments inflicted upon them because stupid people jaywalk into traffic and don't know how to use pavements.

## TRAFFIC LIGHTS

Why do we sit there in the middle of the night with no other cars in sight, waiting for traffic lights to tell us we can go? What the actual fuck is that all about? You'd think by now they could sense traffic and not have you just sitting there like an idiot waiting for the invisible car to drive by.

## HIGH BEAM WANKERS

Do I need to say anything more!! Oi, you behind me, and you approaching me, switch your fkn high beam off you knob jockey!

## DORIS AND ELSIE ARE AT IT AGAIN!

I'm sorry but Doris and Elsie should not be driving when they have been issued a bus pass. It's just not safe, there is no way their reactions are quick enough.

Sunday afternoon drivers tootling along without a care in the world, holding up the traffic and pulling out on a poor unsuspecting passersby because they are wearing their varifocals and need to look straight up or down through them to see properly!

DVLA issuing licences to the over 70's *'what in gods name are you thinking for fucks sake?'*

## PEOPLE WHO DON'T INDICATE

Oh my christ! BMW and Audi wankers, lovely flashy cars but they haven't got a clue what an indicator is for!

Apparently neither do tourists!

*'oh just fuck off!'*


## LEFTHAND DRIVING

It makes no sense! For those of you who drive in the UK, I'm telling you the road system and lefthand driving makes no sense at all. Righthand driving is much more logical. The problem I have with it though is switching between the two. It is a mind bend!

I hold a European driving licence as I live and work between the UK and Spain and I mostly drive on the right. When I am in the UK I am frequently whacking my hand on the driver's door to reach for the gear stick that is clearly now on the left.

I'm mentally saying to myself, the driver should be closest to the middle of the road, just to sanity check I'm on the right side of the road. Then there's a car coming straight for me and FUCK, I'm on the wrong side again!

Left-hand driving just causes the need for far too many traffic lights and roundabouts. For anyone who drives in Swindon, wow the highways agency loves a roundabout in Swindon, don't they? WTF is it with all the roundabouts?

## PEOPLE WHO DON'T SAY THANK YOU!

When you have slowed down to purposely let someone out, or to let someone cross the road when they are clearly not at a crossing and attempting to jaywalk their way across the road. And then the ungrateful bastards don't flash or raise a hand to say thank you.

I find myself shouting *'you're fucking welcome'*, a quick acknowledgement costs nothing and relieves the stresses of people like me who slow down and stop for everyone!

People who don't say thank you I'm gifting you the *'Prick'* award

## PARKING

Are you one of those knob jockeys who park over two spaces at the supermarket or retail park? Heads on into a space with a deliberate slant on to prevent another car from parking next to you?

This is me! I am that knob jockey, in the back corner of Asda over two spaces because there is no way Doris knows how to park that fucking Volvo Estate she's cruising around town in.

I know it pisses people right off that's why I go up the corner to do it. I don't want my car doors scratched and dented by people who just don't give a shit about anyone else's property.

I'll award myself the *'knob jockey of the year'* for parking!

## CARPARK FEES

In Lanzarote everywhere is free to park except the airport and then we are talking a couple of euros a day, not like the £5 for 5 minutes like UK airports the robbing bastards.

The UK literally fucking robs you blind and monetises fkn everything!

Carpark charges you are awarded the honour of *'what the actual fuck!'*

## MOTORBIKES FILTERING

This pisses me off and I ride a motorbike. I can do it and have done it. Still, when I'm sitting in my car fkn queuing and a motorbike is filtering through the lanes it winds me up.

It's pure jealousy nothing more, they are moving and I'm stuck in a bastard queue!

My fellow bikers 'are you being fucking serious?'

66

# A car's weakest part is the nut holding the steering wheel

UNKNOWN

99

## 6

# TECHNOLOGY

WE HAVE COME SUCH a long way since the days of plugging in a modem and using your BT landline to upload or download files, which took an age and made the most bizarre screeching noise.

Today we have different issues with technology some of which I've rattled off here for you:

## IOS UPDATES

How annoying are they? That circle of doom and progress bar that declares 45-minutes to go 10-minutes before your next zoom call! WTF!

You are just about to go on a meeting or have a full diary and one of these auto updates kicks in before you have a chance to stop it. Or something stops working because until you've completed the update it's no longer compatible with your MacBook, phone or iPad! It drives me insane.

My computer only plays up on days I need it to perform like a finely tuned formula one car.

I'm currently running on macOS Monterey 12.6 the 12.3 version upgrade I took a couple of weeks ago knocked GarageBand and audacity offline so I struggled to edit audio for a couple of days until their bug fix and 12.6 was released. The desktop version of WhatsApp stopped as well. They fix one thing and break code in another so these releases are never-ending.

IoS updates I annoyingly throw my arms in the air to you and declare '*You must be fucking joking!*'

## NORTON & MCAFEE SUBSCRIPTIONS

Microsoft and the annoying flaws purposely built into them to make money from you! Do you really think virus protection is needed? Apple products don't need them. I've never once needed to protect my MacBook and buy endless virus subscriptions to keep my laptop working and my data safe and protected!

I swear to god this is a Bill Gates by design business model. Build an operating system susceptible to viruses and then we make our money not from the device but from the software needed to protect the device. My theory is he practised with technology and then decided to move this model to the human race, and no one is going to convince me otherwise! - see Chapter 9.

Bill Gates you sir are a 'C U Next Tuesday!'

## CHARGING CABLES & PHONE BATTERY LIFE

My phone is on charge, and there's only one cable in sight, all of a sudden my phone is no longer on charge and someone else's phone is? WTF is that all about?

Do they wander over and determine 26% that's fine, charge their own phone then don't plug yours back in when they are done? It's so bloody annoying, it's a bit like sharing your chips - NO just stop it, get your own chips and your own goddamn charging cable!

Battery life on mobile phones, seriously does apple send some kind of secret code to the battery to say drain as soon as we get to two versions of the iPhone ahead? My phone has gone from an 8-hour life span to 30 minutes at best, it's constantly on charge!

Charging cables and mobile phone battery life - *'what the fucking fuck?'*

## WIFI

Oh just fuck off, no signal! WTF are you talking about 5 minutes ago I had a full signal now just as I'm about to go on a call my VPN has kicked me out and says 'no internet!'

Why? Why does it always happen at important moments? How can you go from everything working like a dream to has wifi even been invented yet or shall I plug my dial-in modem back in!

Slow internet, you are getting the honour of *'Are you being fucking serious?'*

## POP-UP ADS

OMG, I'm straight off that fucking website when these annoying fuckers pop up. It really irritates the hell out of me when I think I've clicked the cross but it actually opened the advert, and now I'm on a fucking random website selling shite!

*'Just fuck off!!!'*

## FORGOTTEN PASSWORD

Enters the password, computer says, *'you can fuck off you're not logging in to today Jo you tosspot!'*

Are you fucking kidding me!!! Don't do this to me now FFS, I'm on a zoom in ten minutes and you're not letting me in, give me a break!

Ok compose yourself Jo, try every password you can think of before it locks your account. Nope none of them work. Ok password recovery let's do this.

Please answer the following question - what was the name of your first pet? FML did I put my first family pet as a child or did I put my first pet when I left home, the sweat is dripping from my forehead now and the rage is boiling inside me.

Ok, I'm in, now to set a new password: ERROR! 'F*k off jo you can't enter a password you've already used!'* What?!?!?!? are you actually being fucking serious!!! Just let me fkn in, I'm going to be late.

Sets password to FUCKoFFYoUTW4T!! I'm that annoyed at this point.

## SLOW DOWNLOADS

I pay for the fastest speed of fibre optic broadband, it makes no difference though. When it's something important and I need it to happen in an instant. Like an IoS update, so I can carry on using my laptop, I need speed not dawdling along downloads. It's not happening, it is like my internet just goes on strike.

*'Fuck my actual life!'*

## PRINTER ISSUES

Every time I need to print something off, one of six things happens to me, there could be more;

- The printer jams
- The ink runs out
- The printer head isn't aligned so it prints off all blurred

- I've run out of paper
- Cannot connect to the printer it's not on your network
- It prints off (9/10 this doesn't happen)

*'I fucking hate printers!'*

## ACCIDENTALLY DELETING SOMETHING IMPORTANT

My work here is done, I click close and my heart instantly sinks FML I forgot to save it first. I realise my error within a split second.

Oh no, what the fuck have I done??? Nooooooo, come back, come back!

*'FML I sound like Rose from Titanic!'*

## THE "BLUE SCREEN OF DEATH"

*'Oh just fuck off I hate you!'*

## CAN'T OPEN EMAIL ATTACHMENTS

'Oh just fuck off I hate you as well!'

## INSUFFICIENT DISK SPACE / MEMORY

*And you knob jockey, you are the bane of my fucking life!!*

I pay £2.79 a month for extra fucking storage on my phone that's not used, I've got 10TB of space on dropbox and iCloud how can there not be enough fucking space?? Just fuck off!

## "THERE IS A PROBLEM WITH THIS WEBSITE'S SECURITY CERTIFICATE"

*'For the love of god! Just fucking take me there!'*

## AUTO CORRECT

My WhatsApp messages always make sense until I press send and mid-send, in the airways, WhatsApp and Messenger do something to them to make me look an absolute moron or pissed 24/7!

I have given up on the word 'What' it always translates to 'Why' and 'Gave' magically becomes 'Have' and vice versa!

My worst text was when I told my husband *'I won't be long I'm just w\*nking Louis by the seafront'.*

This is Louis I can assure you I was definitely not w*nking him by the seafront nor in this photo! He might be a good boy but this would be a step too far!

I have included a few of the internet's finest text and auto-correct fails for your sheer WTF pleasure, enjoy!

Having a hard time sleeping. Trying to find the right relaxation sound to lul me into lala land. I'm thinking genital thunderstorm, what do you think?

Oh god. Genital

Genital

Genital

Wtf!!

Genital

Ahhhhhh

---

Odd request but can I use your little fan?

I think I'm getting dick and our room is sooooo hot

SICK

God

I'M LAUGHING

Of course!

Thank you! And omg that one wtf phone

XDDDDD

---

HEY DUDE

I GOT A NEW PENIS TODAY!!!

... PENIS!*

PENIS!*

OMFG

***PC***

K.

=]

---

Great news - Grandma is homosexual!

Okay?

Homo hot lips

Hot tulips

I am getting fisted now

Frustrated

Grandma is h o m e

from h o s p i t a l

Hahaha homo hot lips!!??

---

Chicken vaginas sound good for dinner?

No...not really.

And...ROFL btw

? What would you rather have?

Omg, hahahaha! Chicken fajitas. Wtf, phone!

Definitely not chicken vaginas.

Oh ... that sounds much better :p

---

You should bring the fan up and fuck me in.

Fuck. I meant tuck.

I choose the former

118

**66**

# The saddest aspect of life right now is that science gathers knowledge faster than society gathers wisdom.

ISAAC ASIMOV

# POLITICS

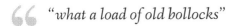 *"what a load of old bollocks"*

THEY ARE an entitled bunch of absolute knob jockeys. I wouldn't vote for any of them right now!

I've always held conservative principles but as it stands today they wouldn't get my vote.

A general election to let the people decide who they want to run the country is needed to restore some confidence, or better still scrap the whole thing and start again with something new. Sooner rather than later, before we're all homeless through mortgage interest rate leaps, winter fuel bill rises, and a cost of living crisis no one can afford.

Not to mention the health crisis caused by their dire covid-19 management. 165,000 vacancies in Health and Social Care sector, almost 39,000 in the NHS with over 13,000 beds being blocked because there is nowhere to release them to from the hospital.

7-million people on NHS waiting lists - 7 FKN MILLION!!!

40,000 care workers were sacked and vilified for not getting their shitty vaccine on the basis that they were all selfish C U Next Tuesdays, and killing granny. This is despite the fact that for 18 months we were encouraged to clap like a bunch of fukwits on our front doorsteps in appreciation of them supposedly risking their own lives. What thanks did they get? The UK government sacked them.

This was followed months later by an admission from Pfizer that they never tested the vaccine's ability to stop transmission despite that being the narrative spewed every day. The vaccine never has and never did stop transmission it was all lies.

What a bloody shambles!

You can sign the #togetherdeclaration here >> **Open Letter: "Apologise, Reinstate, Compensate 40,000 care sector workers forced out"**

I'm just watching Sky News and the chap from the Economist has just asked "does Liz Truss have the shelf life of a lettuce?" 🤣🤣🤣.

Today as I write this she's thrown Kwasi Kwarteng under the bus for a mini-budget they came up with together, which the Bank of England has had to stump up £65billion for in bonds, the economy looks set to nose dive into a recession and we the people are paying for this game of monopoly.

Nicola Sturgeon to Sky News, 'If Liz Truss phoned me today, I'd tell her to resign along with the rest of her government.'

It's car crash TV and if it wasn't plunging people into poverty it would be funny.

British politics I award you the honour of 'C U Next Tuesday's'

A few days have passed since I started writing this chapter.

We now have Jeremy ~~C~~Hunt as our fourth chancellor this year. He has come in like a steamroller and reversed the majority of Kwasi and Liz's disastrous mini-budget.

Liz Truss sent Penny Mordant into the wolves for Prime Minister's Questions, she literally didn't turn up for PMQ, it was embarrassing and such a sign of weakness. She later wandered in all sheepish.

What a week it's been!!

Liz truss lasted 44 days in office and we now await our fourth prime minister in two years the third in the past 3 months. I have jars of mustard in my fridge that have a longer shelf life!

Babies born earlier this year have so far lived through, two monarchs, four chancellors, three prime ministers, three health ministers, and two home secretaries!

The Tory backbenchers are now saying 'Bring Back Boris" - they love a good slogan don't they? Boris is wearing his bright red Bermudas in the Dominican Republic and now preparing to cut his holiday short! Only 60 days ago his party ousted him, now they are crying for his forgiveness and want him back! If Boris gets back to number ten he will be the second prime minister to achieve this extraordinary task.

"Get ready for Rishi" is gearing up his campaign again (god help us all!) I'm going to come back to this chapter as soon as we have a new prime minister apparently on 28th October in 4 days' time.

## 25th October update

Rishi Sunak is the new prime minister! It's like the fucking hokey jokey! Good grief the eyes of the world are watching all of this and must collectively be thinking WTAF!

Meanwhile over in the USA sleepy Joe Biden is celebrating the UK's new Prime Minister Rasheeee Sanoook. My deepest sympathies to all the sane people of the USA.

This man needs some bed socks, a hot chocolate and a rocking chair FFS he is an embarrassment! I swear the senate is just taking the piss now. He can hardly string a sentence together.

So we now have two puppets from the WEF in the main jobs at numbers 10 and 11 Downing Street, revolving doors should be fitted for convenience to get one in and one out quicker!

As witnessed already, the markets control us not the cabinet! As long as they're happy the people will never have their democracy.

Let the circus continue, I live in hope that one day the people will collectively fully awaken.

66

# Politicians and diapers should be changed frequently and all for the same reason.

JOSÉ MARIA DE EÇA DE QUIEROZ

# FREEDOM OF SPEECH

### No Trigger Warning Needed I Was Censored

## CANCEL CULTURE

SEE all of the above in this chapter, oh no wait it got cancelled, for fear of me being cancelled, and committing career suicide. The irony! I'm not best pleased about it, but hey, I don't want to offend anyone and be accused of bigotry, do I? I'm already 8 chapters deep I might have offended people already, it's perhaps too late to turn back now.

What I can say is I have differing views on many topics that some people wouldn't agree with (actually most people do agree with, but are fearful of the woke mob cancelling them too so they choose to remain mute). I'd be happy to sit and have a civilised conversation with anyone if I had a view and understanding of the topic they wanted to discuss.

When I say I don't want to cause harm or offend I mean it, so I agreed to remove it.

Sadly I now have a mortgage to pay because a con woman we will just call her a C*NT, for now, stole my life savings.

The sad truth is if you disagree with the woke mob then you will get vilified and cancelled. For me, the absolute lack of my views on some big topics in this chapter is a testament to how true this statement is and how much people now live in fear of other people. It's a very sad frustrating world we live in.

We are no longer allowed a difference of opinion, the mob would hound you for differing opinions and close you down. Only their viewpoint is valid and that is the point I guess I wanted to make.

So long as we live in a world that encourages the labelling of groups and segregation of people, LGBTQ, Black, White, CIS, Christian, Muslim, Right-wing, Left-wing, Off their tits on weed wing, there will always be a divide and hatred and cancelling will be encouraged.

How did we forget we are a human race and our blood runs the same colour? I honestly couldn't care less what or who you are, what religion you are, what colour your skin is, how you identify, dress or who you sleep with, it's none of my business.

If you have green or yellow blood and you are in fact a descendant of ET then I might sit up and pay attention. Otherwise, crack on, just be happy and let me do the same!

> "We don't need labels we just need to get on and spread love not hate!"
>
> — JO GILBERT

If your blood is red you are my people, you are welcome in my circle, my friendship group, and my home! (for fucks sake don't just turn up unannounced though as that pisses me right off. Also if you do happen to be a JW, please respect I'm an atheist so I don't need you to peddle your beliefs onto me, no amount of clock tower magazine is going to change that. If we can agree on that point you are welcome too!)

Let's take Queue Gate - Philip Schofield and Holly Willoughby both marred in controversy recently and scrutinised by thousands of people who are trying to get them cancelled for supposedly jumping a queue to pay respects to the Queen, when the narrative whether true or not was they were working.

WTAF is wrong with people trying to get them cancelled!!!

I would hazard a guess they mainly preach #bekind on a Monday and hang them on a #Tuesday, it's ludicrous. I'd also stake a few quid on the fact that most of them would probably have queue jumped too given half the chance. I know I would have if there had been a way to get 'priority boarding' treatment as millions do every day for flights, and if I could be arsed to even queue in the first place, it's utter hypocrisy.

Now, let's assume they weren't working and used their privileges of being on TV to get in via a side door for journalists. Their actions didn't affect anyone else in the queue, if a journalist was waiting to go in they may have affected them for a few minutes, but definitely not the general public.

And the question here is 'so what?' So they made an unpopular choice, for this particular woke mob. It doesn't give them the right to get them fired and cancelled. Just fuck off with your cancel culture, despite your opinion mine and others' opinions are valid too.

For the record, I admire that celebrities like David Beckham, James Blunt and Tilda Swinton queued with the public, all credit to them, however, let's not forget they shit on a toilet every day as we do, the only difference is, they are well known and earn more than most people. So why shouldn't they queue, they are people just the same as everyone else.

Cancel culture you are getting a WTF score of '*get a fucking life.*'

## CENSORSHIP

The irony, I am not allowed free speech in my own book, hence this chapter has been heavily censored.

Here are a few things that will definitely get you shadow-banned online, in Meta jail or de-platformed.

- Swearing or talking in a way Facebook thinks you're being a twat to someone
- Not being a twat to anyone but Facebook thinks you are indeed a twat
- Talking about CONVID, '*coughs*' sorry Covid, or the jibby jabby jab thing they want everyone to have
- Talking about the earth being flat
- Talking about politics that they don't agree with
- Answering the question 'What is a woman'
- Sharing a photo of bare skin - is considered nudity and porn
- Mentioning Donald Trump
- Sharing a video taking the piss out of sleepy Joe Biden (on a serious note and for hours of entertainment if you search #joebiden on TikTok its car crash viewing)

I could go on but you know what I mean here. Online censorship by the elite and government is getting out of control. If it's not their narrative (clearly, that is the only one allowed), then you are not getting a voice and will be put in jail, de-platformed and banned. Fact!

What you can share and get away with as it pops up on my newsfeed quite regularly:

- Animal cruelty
- Racism
- Child abuse
- Cloned accounts
- Violent videos of women and men being attacked
- Encouraging children to commit suicide
- Encouraging children to physically change gender

Censorship you are getting a *'who the fuck do you think you are? You are censoring the wrong stuff!!'*

Let's not forget the stats here of what else they are not stopping, while they distract you with viruses and war. They are diverting your attention away from:

- The **800,000 children** who go missing every year!

- Human trafficking generating over **$100billion annually!** Human trafficking generates more money than drugs and illegal firearms combined!
- There are approx. **30 million slaves** worldwide and **10 million** of them are **children!**

Paypal - cancelling accounts of any group with a differing opinion or fighting for their rights. Big tech and the government censoring us all with their own narrative.

The online safety bill - *'oh just fuck off!'* that's not about safety it's about one narrative and one narrative only, and if you don't agree with their narrative you are de-platformed.

I am scoring you the honour of *'What a fucking bunch of cockwombles'*.

**66**

# I may not agree with what you have to say, but I will defend to the death your right to say it.

FRENCH WRITER, WIT, AND
PHILOSOPHER VOLTAIRE

# THE SCAMDEMIC AKA COVID 19

### Trigger Warning! Difference of Opinion Incoming

I'M NOT EVEN sure I can muster up the energy to even write about the shit storm that has happened since 2019 ended. I cannot pretend it didn't happen and share my view. I woke in January 2020 and the world had gone fucking mental! I seriously thought I was tripping from a new years eve spike!

 "What a load of old bollocks, for fucks sake can we get a fucking rewind or skip to the good parts?"

— JO GILBERT, MOST DAYS SINCE 2019

I may as well just come clean here, although from my previous comments in the book, you've probably already gathered I am not vaccinated and I was branded one of those *'Tin Hat'* wearers as the events of 2020 unfolded. I am so glad that I held fast to my conviction that something was not right and untruths were being told.

I was not responsible for anyone's granny dying and neither were you! If you want to point those fingers of blame here are the grid coordinates to point them to 51.5034° N, 0.1276° W.

The narrative is changing as the data is shared and we can now see the lies for what they were and still are. Exactly that, pure lies. What we have witnessed is a global-scale crime against humanity, a genocide by lockdown and injection which most willingly walked into and complied with. The death toll is not over yet by any stretch of the imagination. The two-year wait lists on the NHS alone are a testament to how many more deaths this shower of shit will cause.

I am qualified in six sigma and I distinctly remember during my initial green belt training the tutor walking into the room and telling a story about his parrot which kept saying;

 "plot the data, plot the data"

— SOMEONE'S PARROT

## How long will it take to realize this?

**Only a fool can be happy to show off a pass for things he used to do without a pass**

So during the beginning of the Scamdemic, that's exactly what I began to do, plot the data. You see data doesn't lie, it has no hidden agenda it's just data. It doesn't vote for any party, it's not part of any conspiracy theory unless of course that data has been manipulated to paint a deceptive picture. The important thing to remember here is the same data can be represented or misrepresented depending on how it is presented.

Let us say for example;

*'The average age of death is 86 'from' covid which is actually higher than the average life expectancy, so it really is good news for the majority of the population.'* - Boris and his cronies particularly Rishi (our new prime minister) could've told you this and not panicked you nor locked you down costing the economy billions and leaving us in the shit storm we are currently in. But they didn't.

Instead, their narrative was something like this;

*'232 died today 'with' covid and it's rising, stay indoors, stay safe, protect the NHS don't kill granny.'* - The control and fear narrative was in play.

Do you see the difference? The same data presented differently gives a different feeling and instils fear.

There's the whole topic of manipulation because of the words 'from' and 'with' to consider as well, you can die 'with' covid from a bungee jump injury gone wrong and they would still record it as a covid death within 28 days of testing positive. The data was without a shadow of a doubt manipulated and presented to you to instil fear and control.

The real raw data tells a very different story to the one we have been spoon-fed for two and a half years, it's there for anyone to go and find, hiding in plain sight. Anyone who spoke out was cancelled, silenced, or de-platformed. That in itself should've set off alarm bells, but still the masses complied.

The problem is people are lazy and most need to be told what to do. They don't use any form of logic to justify or question why they are being asked to do these things. They queued up for jabs so they could get their freedom back and go on holiday with little thought to the longer-term health disadvantages and harm.

Sheila is now on her sixth jab, she's developed a twitch in her right eye, and the left side of her face is dropping, she's got no energy and frequently gets covid - thank god she gets her jab! Can you imagine how ill she would be without it?

God forbid our natural immunity was given a chance as nature intended and not synthetically changed. That would cost the Pharma industry billions and we don't want that do we?

Wear a mask - ok, get a jab - ok, get a Covid certificate - ok, get another jab - ok, download the apps so we can track you - ok. Stay indoors - unless we give you a certificate to tell you that you can work - ok, report your friends and neighbours if they go out - ok, eat out but only until 10pm - ok, you morons you ate out now it is spreading again, now stay indoors - ok. This is my particular favourite wash your hands and sing happy fucking birthday - OKAY!!!

In, out, in, out, spread it all about.

Meanwhile in government offices around the world including Downing Street: Don't watch us, we are not affected. The virus treats us differently you see, we can still party, and we don't need to wear masks where the public can't see us, or on our private jets. The rules are there for the many, not the few. We are Elite and we are lying to you and holding you in fear and you fell for it hook line and sinker!

Do you really think if covid was that deadly the people making the rules and holding all of the data, all of the facts would be throwing parties while your loved ones died on their own? I don't fucking think so!!! They would be living in the same fear, locked away in single-family units like the rest of us.

Covid didn't kill all those old folk, lockdowns, loneliness and DNRs did, they gave up on life! The excess winter deaths were hardly any different than any other year!

It's time the world woke up.

The police issued **126 fines** during the Partygate investigation, including to Boris Johnson and Rishi Sunak. They had all the data, they knew the truth and decided to party regardless **THEY WERE NOT AFRAID OF COVID!**

Can you see the nonsense of it all?

> "If you have the data telling you the virus is deadly, would you be partying with work colleagues? They were **LYING** and holding you in **FEAR!**"

My husband for the 14 years I've known him, never so much has had a sniffle, he was as fit as a fiddle. Sadly, he queued up like millions of others and complied due to peer pressure from his work colleagues and the media to go along and get it done. Two jabs later his memory is severely affected, he can hardly breathe most days, he lives in fear of some kind of heart attack and has hardly any energy.

He's just not the same person he was two years ago. Don't get me wrong he has some really good days, however, that vaccine has taken away many years of what would have been a healthy life, I've never known him to be ill and catching stuff all the time as he does now.

It's not just my husband it's my friends, family members and associates too, some reporting not feeling right since having their doses of the jab, Bell's palsy, myocarditis, blood clots, miscarriages, and constant recurring illness. It makes me so sad and so angry.

One of the reasons we moved to Lanzarote was because of my health and vulnerability to airborne viruses. Having had sepsis twice and pretty much-catching everything going it was time to move away from the damp air to a dry climate. I was a perfect candidate to queue up and get the vaccine. I was offered it in one of the early groups.

I genuinely believe I would not be here today to write this book if I had. I don't know this as a fact clearly and I'm not willing to test the theory either just to leave a note to say I fkn told you so!

Millions were injured and maimed by it, and yet still people are queuing in their droves to pump that shit into themselves and their children. Their own fkn children for god's sake. Without knowing the long-term side effects and damage it can do.

I have watched so many documentaries on the thalidomide tragedy of 1957, nearly 60 years ago now, thalidomide was prescribed to treat morning sickness in pregnant women the side effects at that time were unknown, just like these vaccines. What followed was the biggest man-made medical disaster ever, where over 10,000 children were born with a range of severe and debilitating malformations.

I ask you why the fuck would you be willing to line up for this risk? It's fucking nuts, I fail to make any logical sense of any of it. I'm sorry if this is triggering you because you got jabbed. It triggers me every day because you did too, I'm genuinely concerned for your longer-term health.

I am not an anti-vaxxer, I have had all other vaccines, even those to visit holiday destinations like Hep A and Typhoid shots. My children are all vaccinated, but there was something just off about this my gut instinct was to investigate further. The fear narrative and some contradictions in the media were just a bit too OTT for me.

While the majority of people were consuming the mainstream media frenzy of people dropping dead in the streets whilst wearing masks, blaming China for eating bats and branding them dirty bastards, some of us were looking in the opposite direction of what the agenda could be here.

The World Health Organisation, the World Economic Forum and the Centre for Disease Control with Anthony Fauci and Bill Gates, what were they up to?

Boris Johnson, Chris Whitty, Patrick Vallance, Savid Javid, Rishi Sunak and co, plus other world leaders who are all members of the WEF, mere puppets to the elitist agenda including our now very own King Charles - god help us! He hung out with Jimmy Saville FFS and heads up the WEF!

Anyhow I digress, we all hid in fear of the disease we couldn't see, we didn't see dying loved ones, we missed birthdays, marriages, funerals, and holidays, and we missed out on life and freedom for more than two years. They made you turn on your friends and family, they divided us all into different groups and labelled us! So we did their dirty work for them, and the hate cycle spun some more. (I refer to this in Freedom of Speech)

The shit show is still ongoing in other countries people are actually being held as hostages in their own homes, for no, valid reason and the world stays silent.

This is the biggest load of bollocks I have ever known. The flu magically vanished for two years, I wonder where it went? Every winter people catch colds and winter flu, and every year people die from it. Why now do people test for covid and then photograph their tests like a badge of honour on social media WTF even is this all about?

The tests don't work, and mask-wearing is not effective it's all a load of old bollocks.

There is a much wider agenda in play here, in history, the economy has only ever boomed from War or Pandemics, we now have them both in play it's a perfect storm. And let's not forget the promise to reduce the global population using a vaccine which Bill Gates the self-appointed god, who funds a lot of 'the science' in all of this has developed, and we all know how shit his track record is. Don't believe me go read about his polio vaccine trials or try owning a Microsoft computer without virus protection for more than a month.

Just follow the money - there you will find your answer!

I am glad that I can proudly say I stood on the right side of history in the years that follow as the masses die and this scandal is investigated further by future generations.

I will never forget and never forgive those in power for their abhorrent abuse of their powers, for their forced removal of personal choice and bodily autonomy. MP's and the elite all played their part in mass genocide.

I could go on for hours but I won't, I cannot unsee what I have seen, researched and found. The evidence is grim, we have all been played. We need to come together and say no to this nonsense!

Covid-19 and the governments who pushed it, I am awarding you *'what a load of old bollocks you murdering heartless C U Next Tuesdays!'*

**"**

# Sometimes I wonder if this is all happening because I didn't forward that email to 10 people

UNKNOWN

**"**

# A DAY IN THE LIFE OF MY BEST FRIEND

## Abigail Horne

 **Abigail Horne**
28 m · 🌐

One day I'm going to look back on today, in all it's stupidity and horrendously awful moments... and laugh.

But today is not that day. Today it is not funny, although you would think it was straight out of a comedy sketch.

I will tell you when I can muster a sentence that isn't just filled with "f*cks, what the actual f*cks and oh just f*ck offs"

Today I just need ALL the wine...

#halfterm

147

Try if you will to picture this.

Abi is a self-employed businesswoman working in publishing in the midst of three client book launches this particular week and finishing off the tail end of a new programme launch.

It's half term, she has three kids at home, aged 11, 3 1/2 and 2 years old and two dogs. There are no family members on hand to support her today, her in-laws are not well, her mum is on holiday and her husband is at work.

Abi's house is on the market and the estate agent has called to say a couple are interested in viewing the house today at 5:30pm, they insisted. She tried to put them off because her husband would be home to help tomorrow, but they insisted it had to be today.

So Abi like a boss is on form giving everywhere inside and out a good tidy up, and clean, trying also to keep the toys that are out for the little ones to the bare minimum. She's dealing with broken kitchen door knobs thanks to her 3 1/2-year-old daughter and a Pritt Stick.

Unfazed by all of this Abi sets about lighting a few moments candles to create the right fragrance and ambient mood.

It's 30 minutes before the viewing and her eldest has just started vomiting all over the place. Not in the downstairs loo or the bathroom literally walking around the place throwing up.

Abi suffers from emetophobia (The fear of sick). She now has piles of sick everywhere, he's even somehow managed to throw up on the dog!

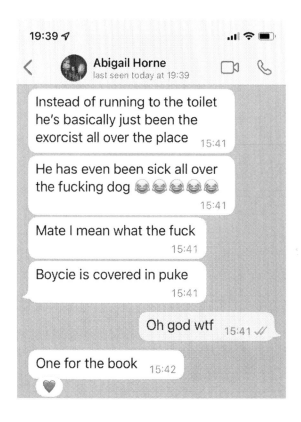

The house has gone from the decadent scent of Bergamot, Jasmine and Freesias to the sour pungent stench of vomit. Right at this very moment, Abi is probably wishing she had opted for a quick blowie instead that Christmas night 11 years ago!

I imagine her thoughts right then were *'fuck my actual fucking life you have got to be fucking kidding me, I'm not cut out for this parenting bullshit!!!'*

She had to ask her husband to come home from work to help! They manage to clean all the sick up and blow some fresh air through the rooms to get rid of the smell and hope the candles work their magic!

Crisis averted, the kids are now sat in the car, the eldest with an empty popcorn bucket as he's still vomiting, and the estate agent and potential buyers turn up. It's time for Abi to get out of the house to let the estate agent do his thing!

There are no less than 53 photos online of Abi's house including every room, the bathroom and a detailed 3d floor plan - you can literally walk around the house via a simulator.

The feedback from the couple viewing it *'our current house has four bathrooms we couldn't possibly go down to one bathroom, we were hoping for an ensuite!*

*'What the actual FUCK!'*

Right you absolute pair of time-wasting knob jockeys you saw the property details, the floor plan and the photos, and you could clearly see it didn't have an ensuite, but you hoped on viewing it in person it might have one - are you fucking ten pence short of a pound mate? WTAF!!!

Estate agents for not thoroughly understanding their client's needs I award you the honour of 'Cockwombles'.

To the couple who went to view it despite knowing all the details, I award you the honour of 'fucking time wasters!'

To Abi's son for his glorious re-play of the exorcist 'nicely played' 😜 x

To Abi, WTF mate you deserve all the Wine I despair for you! 🍷

"

# There's Nothing More Annoying Than Timewasters When You are Selling Your home

UNKNOWN

"

## 11

## EVERYTHING ELSE

To END THE BOOK, I'm rattling off everything here I've missed in other chapters. These are in random order as they popped into my mind.

## UNSOLICITED DIRECT MESSAGES

Here's the sequence:

1. Accept friend requests as friends in common and assume that they must be ok, and not a twat
2. Within 20 seconds or up to 72hours, a message will appear in my DM's
3. Within 30 seconds, 20 plus of my posts have been clicked and liked or 🖤
4. I think oh fuck not another dickhead

5.  I read their message "Hey Jo, Are you having some obstacles with crushing your Sales goals? Take a peek at this 10-sales-a-day Blueprint. I see this is just what you need to move things to the next level for your business. See what other business owners like you have to say. (this is a real example)

6.  I reply "Can you just stop with this unsolicited nonsense? Get out of my inbox with your naff sales message, this is not how sales are done. Whoever is teaching you this nonsense needs to educate themselves. Bore off" (this is exactly my reply)

7.  I block them

8.  Rinse and repeat that about 12 times a week.

Unsolicited DM's, sales messages like above, dick pics, marriage proposals, requests to help with money - '*what the actual fuck*'

## FACEBOOK GROUPS

I currently have over 1000 invitations outstanding to join Facebook groups, probably perfectly amazing groups if you are interested in the group topic. I love that people create groups for a particular audience, what absolutely boils my piss is when someone adds me to a group I didn't choose to go into!

How dare you! (FML I sound like Greta Thunberg).

It's my Facebook account, what makes you think you have any right to just add me to a group without asking me?

'*Are you being fucking serious?*'

## REPLY ALL

There's always one knob jockey isn't there! An email is sent out to a host of thousands and one smart arse hits reply all! Why do people do this?

I award you the honour of '*Prize knob head*!'

## CHILDBIRTH

Vaginal childbirth, fucking stings a bit doesn't it? WTF is that all about? You'd think after the first one, tearing me a new arsehole I'd never go there again!

FML I did it two more times, by the time the third one came around I think I'd probably got the widest foof going, you could fit a fucking combine harvester in it. In fact, I think a farmer I pulled in a bar in 1997 is still in mine wondering where the fuck he parked his!

Thank god for gas and air and stitches is all I'm saying that was one hell of a trauma that needed sewing back together nice and tightly FML!

## VULVA CASTS

Please refer to the above! No one needs to see one of those on my fkn mantle piece or anyone else's either for that matter!!! Nope, no thank you, it's a big fucking NO from me, I am in touch with my femininity but this is a step too far for me, I just don't get it.

I've got YONI tattooed on my left forearm, but I ain't dribbling plaster down there no thank you!

> yoni, (Sanskrit: **"abode," "source," "womb," or "vagina"**) in Hinduism, the symbol of the goddess Shakti, the feminine generative power and, as a goddess, the consort of Shiva. In Shaivism, the branch of Hinduism devoted to worship of the god Shiva, the yoni is often associated with the lingam, which is Shiva's symbol.

It actually put me off going to an event this year. I was all up for going until that got advertised. I was scrolling through Instagram saw an event post and liked it, before even realising what I had just liked. It was the unboxing of a vulva cast, at that point, I was like what the actual fuck have my eyes just watched, no thanks, I'm out. Sorry ladies not for me. It all got a bit too weird.

I don't need my family and visitors witnessing a plaster cast of my vulva to put them off their supper. I imagine the lost farmer would probably pop his head out, smile and say cheese!

*'What in the glorious fuck are you doing that for!!'*

## PELVIC FLOOR

*'I haven't fucking got one!'* Can you imagine I have hay fever, I'm allergic to my three dogs' fur and every time I sneeze, cough or laugh I piss my fucking pants!

What a catch my husband landed when he met me.

Apparently exercising will help, there is a slight problem in that running three steps results in me also pissing myself. Sit-ups, I don't fucking think so vaginal farting and pee it's all too much!

So, Tena Lady, it is! FML, women have all the fun shit to deal with.

## THE MENOPAUSE

As I'm writing this book now it's just turned 1:30 am and I'm only awake because of the dreaded menopause.

Sweat is literally dripping off me, I've never known anything like this in my life. Growing up I was lucky to muster up 'clammy' on the hottest of days. I'm what we call in stoke *'nesh'* translated just means feels cold all the time.

I thought these hot sweats were going to be a refreshing change from being cold all the time FML they are vile. The other day I literally thought I was going to internally combust the heat coming right from my feet in a flush up to the top of my head, swiftly followed by buckets of pouring sweat. I'm reliably informed this could go on for 10 years or more!

It's not just the hot flushes and sweat, it's all the other symptoms too;

- Insomnia (that could be the copious amounts of caffeine I drink)
- Mood swings (I had these pre-menopause, sometimes life and people just piss me off)
- Weight gain (that could be takeouts and wine!)
- Memory loss (that could also be the wine!)
- Irritability (that could just be fukwits and stupid people)

Oh the list just goes on and on, joint pain, brain fog, fatigue - you get the picture.

The menopause I'm awarding you a *"what the actual fuck, give me a fucking break for fucks sake!'*

## KIDS AND THEIR DRESS SENSE

I received a voice clip this morning and halfway through the clip was interrupted by *'No shorts Nancy it's Baltic outside it's like minus 25, kids! why doesn't she just wear what I've told her to put on!'* 😂😂

I could hear Nancy objecting in the background, it tickled me.

My five-year-old grandson lives in his boxers no matter how cold the house is he strips off and wanders about wearing as little as possible. My son was the same at his age.

I love seeing those kids where the parents have given up and just said FUCK IT wear what you like. They are now wearing the weirdest outfits around town they can come up with, like a cross between summer, winter, Marvel Avenger and Halloween all mixed together with fluorescent leg warmers.

*'fucking glorious I love your confidence and innocence be more Polly, Nancy, and Finley!'*

## KFC

I fkn love a KFC, part of the reason I'm so fat is I love a KFC! I can't resist them.

It's my hangover food (have you seen the size of me I'm clearly hungover a lot!) You need to trust me here, 8 hot wings, chips with loads of salt, gravy, and a large coke. Your hangover will be gone in about 30 minutes.

What I don't love however is the size of the regular pots of gravy and coleslaw, it's like they are made for kids or the borrowers. £1.49 for a teaspoon's worth of coleslaw, the robbing bastards!

What really boils my piss though is when you order a large gravy and they don't put it in the bag and you don't notice until you get home, or the delivery is short of it!!! Why? Why is the gravy missing every fucking time!

## SPROUTS

Which tosspot decided to spoil Christmas dinner with sprouts? Who in their right fucking mind thought that a Sunday dinner with dry turkey and sprouts is just what every family needs to bring them closer and cheers them up on this special festive day?

The fucking Christmas Grinch that's who! It's Christmas, eat what fkn you want to what you enjoy - just say NO to sprouts and be strong!

If this meal was so amazing how come we only torture ourselves with it once a year? #justsaying

## DOG SHIT

Dog owners who just leave their pets' 💩💩💩 in public spaces and pavements are just the bloody worst. Pick your dog's shit up, you lazy bastards. Clearly, these people have never had to get a twig and flick the shit out of their boots or their kid's shoes on a walk and do the dreaded grass foot slide for 10 minutes until it's off.

Kids treading in it and not realising then treading the stuff all through the house FFS! This isn't just about the state you are leaving parks and pavements you are ruining carpets!!

I rate dog shit - *'lazy bastards pick your shit up!'*

## OTHER PEOPLES CATS & THEIR SHIT

I'm not a huge fan of cats, I'm especially not a fan of all of my neighbour's cats coming and shitting in my garden every night. If I let my dog out on the loose to go and shit in your garden Janice you'd have something to say!

I have dogs and the frequent visit throughout the night from neighbouring cats set off barking and howling frenzies most nights at 2 am, it is driving me mad! The cheeky git of a neighbour then has the audacity to complain about our dogs barking. It's your fucking cat Janice, I can see it on my ring doorbell, FFS, the bloody thing is taking the piss! Keep your cat out of my property and then we could all get a good night's sleep.

I rate cats and their shit - *'Are you fucking kidding me?'*

## BIN BAGS

It's time to empty the kitchen bin, you tear a new 30l bag off the roll but can you find the fucking opening to it? Can you fuck! The damn things have you stood there for ages until you burst a blood vessel of frustration trying to find the end that opens. Those rolls of black refuse sacks are the worst, they are having a fkn laugh with those!

'Are you fucking joking me!'

## PERFORATIONS / TEAR HERE

On yoghurt tubes, cheese strings, pot noodle sauce sachets, ketchup sachets and milk on flights. You fkn liars, 99% of the time those fuckers do not tear and when they do you just end up with shit or powder or suace all over the place and squirted on your clothes! *'For fucks sake!'*

## TOILET ROLL

The era of Mrs Hinch and now everyone's toilet roll flap being stamped with a tap! Just fucking stop it! WTF is wrong with you? You're not a fucking hotel trying to prove it's a new roll since the last guests were in there, it's your family bathroom or toilet for goodness sake.

Here's what happens when visitors sit down to take a pee and reach for the loo roll;

> *'Oh Fuck My Life, it's stamped, WTF, now I'm going to spoil it.... Shazzz! FFS!'*

Also, who are you fkn weirdo's who flap backwards?

*TwitterDavid Sr. on Twitter: "@thistallawkgirl People who don't put the toilet paper roll on right https://t.co/ rxJpiY1xbv" / Twitter*

And the monster who just plonks a new roll on top of the cardboard inner, and doesn't replace it properly WTF how do you even sleep at night?

## PACKAGING

**Cucumbers** - why are cucumbers wrapped in plastic? It's got a perfectly well-designed fucking thick skin given to it by nature, which fucking moron came up with lets condom shrink wrap it that will piss Jo off!

**Fruit and Veg -** in general, that's excessively wrapped in polystyrene and plastic, FML you've taken away my McDonald's plastic straw but that's ok because my fucking bananas have a plastic sleeping bag and tray all of their own!

**Brie** - cardboard box, shrink-wrapped plastic, tinfoil paper! Three fucking layers of packaging to get through for my midnight snack.

Allow me to indulge you in the injury I sustained opening fkn Brie!!! Jesus, it's like completing a task on the crystal maze, it's nearly morning and I've nearly bled to death by the time I've managed to open the damn thing!

**Christmas toys** - oh just fuck off! Plastic, twine, cardboard and some fucking clever CU Next Tuesday in their infinite wisdom decided to add screws as well! We will only have a screwdriver small enough to get them, bastards, out, after Christmas dinner when the crackers have been pulled!

**Corner peel here** - All fucking lies, my ham isn't opening no matter how much I'm pulling, I used to pull blokes faster than I can open a packet of ham FFS!

## CORPORATE PERSONAL DEVELOPMENT PLANS - AKA THE PDP

In my early career years, I was asked to sit a Mensa test by my line manager.

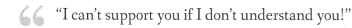 "I can't support you if I don't understand you!"

She was so desperate to 'fix' me and find a course for me to go on. I agreed to do it to shut her up, I popped out a 147 result.

The more she tried to get me a PDP that worked for her and completed her task list, the more I pushed back.

Can you imagine someone setting you a 6 months PDP relative to your annual bonus and you delivering all the tasks on it within two months, she then sets about setting you a whole shed load more because you work at ten times the capacity of everyone else on the team.

She needed to tick those boxes and said the original targets weren't stretched enough! *'Oh just fuck off you tosspot!'*

I'm not a statistic and didn't need a PDP forced on me I had my own for my career and you and your shitty Mensa test were never part of it!

Managers and their tick lists because they don't know how to lead - *'how in the glorious fuck did you even get this role?'*

## NO REPLY

When you send a message to someone, you can clearly see it has been read and they don't reply! This seriously winds me up. You have just fkn read it how hard would it be to quickly reply?

I can see the double blue ticks, I know you've read the message!! Stop being a lazy fkn tosspot!

It's the same with text messages and emails, why do people take days to respond? Is it that they are super unorganised and I'm not, or is it that they are in fact ignorant tosspots?

## PERCEPTION

If I've had this said to me once it's been said a thousand times;

 "Perception is reality"

Do you know what my response is? Your perception is not my reality so sod off! My reality is my reality not your perception of it. Off you trot knob head.

- *'You have tattoos, you can't possibly be professional or any good at what your do.'* - You look like a useless wanker is my perception correct?
- *You have short hair you must be a lesbian* - Seriously? Just fuck off!
- *'You are too outspoken and not politically correct.'* -well hello 👋 If you hadn't realised by now, I don't give a fuck?

People pushing perception and their reality - *'what the actual fuck'*

## THE COST OF GAS & ELECTRICITY

Well, what a shower of shit the energy markets are in! I dedicated 23 years of my life to the UK energy sector and in August 2022 decided enough was enough! OFGEM, BEIS, Kwasi (at the time) fucking cockwombles the lot of them! Couldn't manage a piss-up in a brewery!

Even if you consume zero energy in the UK right now, your annual energy bill for gas and electricity would be approx. £273!

It has reached the point where families can no longer afford to heat their homes this winter. The UK government, Ofgem and BEIS have failed the UK population in delivering sufficient renewable energy measures. They have had years to sort this out, they were warned at least 10 years ago that this would happen. However, they turned a blind eye and only focussed on firefighting the here and now.

They have archaic political barriers, knee-jerk policy reactions with little thought and a blind disregard for the advice shared with them by the sector and its experts.

Look at smart meters, I first started working on that programme in 2006, and they still haven't finished the fkn rollout of them yet, 16 years later!!

They all need to be stuck in a bag and shaken up! They are nothing short of a lying bunch of self-righteous tosspots!

## STRIKES

I'm all for supporting people who need to strike to be seen and heard, however!!!! If you are going to strike and block roads, target the general public, and destroy property then you have no support from me you are a C U Next Tuesday!

The rail strikes this year purposely targeted the weekend of the London Marathon and they expected public support. Oh just fuck off, you targeted an event which supports the Third Sector and much-needed fundraising.

*'You don't half pick your fkn moments to fight you knob jockeys.'*

## DO YOU WANT CHIPS?

I do not like sharing my food. So stop fkn reaching over and pinching chips off my plate as soon as it arrives.

Mums of pensionable age are terrible for this.

 "I'll just pinch a chip"

Just fuck off!!! If you wanted chips why didn't you fkn order some?

My pet hate when eating out in a restaurant is I'm a slow eater, I take my time, so usually, my husband finishes before me and then starts staring at my food like a stray dog. I can be halfway through my steak and he's already eyeing up the veg and chips on my plate.

More often than not he orders some random shit and then wishes he had ordered what I got instead, so we end up swapping and I get to eat a meal I didn't want. To avoid this happening I started ordering everything with blue cheese sauce because he doesn't like it or we order portions just for sharing. Better still I order for him so he's guaranteed to get a good meal and leave mine alone.

As Smithy would say;

66 "Chicken bhuna, lamb bhuna and prawn bhuna, mushroom rice, a bag of chips, keema naan and 9 poppadoms. I bet Pete's already eyeing up my Bhuna! Am I wrong Pete, am I wrong?'

People who assume they can share your chips or have some of your Bhuna when they could've ordered their own 'Knob jockeys'.

## MORBIDLY OBESE PEOPLE ON TRAINS AND PLANES

Let's get this straight the average seat width on an economy short-haul flight is 17-22 inches depending on the plane. Here's what you need to do when booking your flight. Sit your ass down and measure its width if it's more than 17 inches you need to book two seats.

I paid for all of my seat not half of it, and I sure as hell don't want to touch sweaty thighs for four hours!

I have been known to book a whole row so I don't have to sit next to anyone, never mind squishing up by the window against you for hours, no thank you! You are probably very lovely but I don't want to give up half my seat and be uncomfortable the whole journey.

The same rules apply for trains, either book two seats or stand up. I don't need you encroaching on my seat space.

Morbidly obese travellers who plonk themselves on my lap, I award you the honour of *'Fuck my actual life, no, book two seats!'*


## THE BRITISH WEATHER

*'Are you being fucking serious give me a break!'*

We all know how shit the British weather is. However, it is not as shit as the government's ability to manage the implications of such varying weather enabling the good old British public to just get on with their lives. (I've gone there, I've gone political).

**It rains and rains** - we get floods everywhere because rivers are not dredged properly and flood defences are not sufficient or built at all. It's not like we don't know it rains a lot in the Uk, FML there is something not quite right somewhere.

Imagine the jobs to be created from just forward planning for weather defences like rain, heat and snow? Too simple!

**The odd bursts of sunshine** - We close schools and tell people to stay indoors because its too hot - *'oh just fuck off Boris'* Janice pack a picnic love it is time to head off to Brighton or Blackpool, grab a couple of deck chairs, stick a hanky on our heads and get a 99. Lovely!

**Snow** - The country is in turmoil, trains don't run, schools close, roads aren't cleared. *'what a shower of shit, couldn't manage a piss-up in a brewery. Try watching Ice Truckers you might get a few tips FFS.'*

**It doesn't rain for two weeks -** Hose pipe ban!!! *'Stop using all our water you tosspots or we will run out.'* Are you being fkn serious have you seen how much rain falls in the Uk!!! We are an island surrounded by water

FFS. 71% of the earth's surface is covered in the dam stuff, I'm not buying into this bullshit.

## ESTATE AGENTS

I've had my fill of estate agents as you can probably imagine having been ripped off big time by one. My level of trust in them is below zero. So when I'm looking at purchasing a property and it says 'offers over' I can't help but imagine in what other situation would a sane person have a guess at how much something is worth.

Offers over, what does that even mean? Can you imagine going into a garage to buy a car and every windscreen said to offer over the windscreen advertised price, it's crazy is what it is?

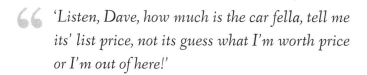

> *'Listen, Dave, how much is the car fella, tell me its' list price, not its guess what I'm worth price or I'm out of here!'*

Then we have those estate agents that come to your house to value it for sale. Having never even stepped one foot in it before and they bring with them printed-off details of *'comparable'* properties.

Comparable, Janice how the fuck do you know it's comparable? You've never stepped foot in here before and have no idea what we've done to it. No Luv, it's nothing like Mrs Matthews down the road who hasn't seen a DIY store in 50 years.

Estate agents for making assumptions about property values, causing negative equity for buyers and asking them to guess the price I rank you - *'What in the glorious fuck are you talking about?!?'*

## CONVEYANCING SOLICITORS

Why the fuck does your own solicitor make you feel like you are a money launderer during your purchase process?

I've never understood why we pay our own solicitors to make us feel like a criminal and riddled with guilt for absolutely no reason whatsoever. Apparently, we pay them to act on behalf of our mortgage provider, I hadn't actually cottoned on to what a fkn joke that was until recently.

The banks and buildings societies have us pay our solicitor to prove to them we aren't criminals. The banks with all the money make us pay to do their due diligence for them - WTF.

I started at one point this year questioning my own sanity in case I had accidentally money laundered a few million quid for someone as part of a massive drug dealing gang and then forgot because I'm menopausal.

Part of the reason, I actually cancelled the purchase of a house earlier this year was because my solicitor was line by line asking questions about my bank statement. FML I've never felt so violated in my life, she knew how many take-outs I ate a week and could no doubt see my Ann Summers order for a rampant rabbit, yoni eggs and three tubes of minty gel!

I was innocent, but now being made to feel guilty for no reason. I lost my temper as she interrogated me over payments into my account. I'm no fraudster, I am currently a victim to fraud, and I didn't like how she was making me feel one bit - the emotion was raw. She made me feel that bad, I asked her if she was a member of the Gestapo. I felt abused!

Solicitors and the money laundering checks I'm going to award you a - *'what the actual fuck!'*

## SPEEDOS

Budgie smugglers worn by the older population should be banned. Seeing someone's granddad wander down the beach with his bed snake swinging around is not a sight I want to see whilst I'm taking in the Vitamin D rays. My lunch almost came up 😖. Good grief the ballsack on them is hanging like a turkey's neck, as they parade right along the water's edge.

Did you know in France, there is a law dating back to 1903 when longer swimming shorts were banned by the Government? Men are forced to wear budgie smugglers in public pools by law. You can not enter a public pool wearing Bermuda-type shorts - apparently a hygiene law.

Speedos on the over 40's no just stop it! - *'what a load of old bollocks.'*

## TRAINS

Trains in the UK I have lots of issues with them:

- Hardly ever on time
- Frequently cancelled - due to strikes, leaves, rain, snow, sunshine, and ice.
- I can buy flights to Europe for €30, yet it costs me £165 to get to London from Stoke.
- At peak times they are overcrowded and standing room only
- When you book a seat someone is always sitting in it
- The toilets stink

## LIFTS

For fucks sake let me get out before you start trying to get in with your pushchair, struth woman, give me strength!

## PEOPLE ON VIDEO CALLS WHO DON'T MUTE THEIR MIC!

You're on a video conference with lots of other people and can't be arsed to just press mute on your microphone, so everyone else is echoing, and there's feedback and we can hardly hear who's speaking!

Learn some meeting and webinar etiquette for god's sake!

I was on a meeting once when the Head of IT just got up and went for a pee in his downstairs loo not closing the door behind him. We couldn't see him he had turned his camera off thank god but forgot to switch his microphone off.

A training session in the evening and a couple had a blazing row over her being on the call and he wanted to watch tv. Seriously zoom is lethal use it with care!

## PAPER STRAWS

Are you being serious? Getting rid of plastic straws was how we are going to solve the issue of plastic waste in the oceans. Really?

I tell you what you've done, you've spoilt my Mcdonald's milkshake is what you've done!

## TOILET SEATS

They should always be down, including the lid, it's designed to keep the germs in the toilet, not in your bathroom.

If you've pee'd on the seat men or women wipe the bloody thing it's not difficult. Stop leaving your pee for other people to clean up!

If you are one of those people leaving toilets public or otherwise in a right state you are gross!

*'Are you being fucking serious?'*


## PEOPLE PUTTING COATS AND BAGS ON VACANT SEATS

This really gets my backup! People are standing up on a packed train and loads, not just one, loads of commuters think it's ok to stick their bag or coat on the seat next to them to avoid having to sit next to someone else. Selfish C U Next Tuesday!

If this is you - you are an utter tosspot! Show some consideration for other commuters. *'We've all had a fkn hard day in the office Andrew, so move you fkn briefcase you tosser!'*

I award you the honour of being a *'Train Wanker!'*

## THE WORD PHONICS

Ever wonder why kids struggle with grasping how to read? Even the word phonics doesn't begin with an F and for this reason, it deserves a *'phucking'* mention in this WTF book!

## DEPRESSION 'MY MENTAL HEALTH'

People pretending to be depressed, just to get time off! - the lowest of lowlifes! There are people who genuinely struggle with their mental health and depression, and sadly there are some who just play the system.

I literally despise these people, the ones who call in sick because they are 'depressed' they aren't really they are just fkn skiving! If sick pay wasn't available they wouldn't be depressed, they would be at work. It's the con of the 21st century!

I know someone who used to factor their sick pay allowance into each year's annual leave, they literally used it as an extra holiday every year they understood the rules and milked it for all it was worth. Using depression as the root cause.

If you are one of these people, you are everything that is wrong with the world! I award you the honour of *'lowlife fkn scumbag!'*

## WORLD MENTAL HEALTH AWARENESS DAY

Where were you all during covid and lockdowns? All, you mental health organisations and advocates, you went deafly silent for 2 years!

This really pisses me off that on days like this every man and their dog all of a sudden care and post about it, but then, silence, fuck all until another celebration day pops up. What about the other 364 days of the year, where are you reminding people each week about mental health awareness, where are you when it's not trending?

I'll tell you where you are...probably jumping on the back of another trending day like 'cancer awareness day' or 'international women's day' just using the day for likes and shares and as a marketing tool.

It makes me sick! If this is you using it for likes and shares *'what a load of old bollocks.'*

## AND FINALLY

I am going to award the final 'call out' of this book to all of the complainers out there. You know the ones they are fkn moaning about everything in life but never come up with a solution. They just bring you their problems and moan and think the world owes them a living!

Fucking hell they are an energy drain, just fuck off! '*Stop moaning start doing ffs!*'

**"**

# Truth hurts. Maybe not as much as jumping on a bicycle with a seat missing, but it hurts.

—LT. FRANK DREBIN (LESLIE NIELSEN), NAKED GUN 2½: THE SMELL OF FEAR

# AFTERWORD

I hope you've enjoyed this book.

I sincerely hope you also managed to disagree with me on some points, or agree with me too. I hope in reading my WTF moments it has conjured your own memories and thoughts whilst reading my musings.

More importantly, I hope you heard your own voice and your own opinions as you read the pages. We might share some views, but we might not.

It matters not.

What matters is we can laugh about them, and discuss them as loving caring human beings. With no hate incited.

**It is better to be hated for what you are than to be loved for something you are not.**

ANDRE GIDE

# ABOUT THE AUTHOR

Jo has been a self-employed Business Consultant and Success Mentor since March 2010. since then she has worked with several large corporations in interim executive roles.

Jo has also supported micro and self-employed business entrepreneurs as an extra pair of eyes on their businesses.

Jo's focus in UK energy for the past 23 years has been business creation, mergers and acquisitions mainly in £100million+ per annum revenue companies in highly regulated markets. Covering operational set-up, business planning and strategy, customer journeys, revenue and profit margins and growth, operational and service excellence, and driving performance via automation, AI and progressive technology.

Throughout Jo's 35-year career, she has trained and become an accredited Mindfulness and Meditation teacher, certified NLP master practitioner, NLP personal development coach, NLP life coach, NLP self-esteem and confidence coach and also a Hypnosis practitioner.

Jo is also qualified in Lean & Agile projects, a Prince2 Practitioner, a Green Belt in Six Sigma, and a practitioner in DMAIC (Define, Measure, Analyse, Improve, Control).

In 2018 Jo published her book 'Strength and Power' and has since gone on to co-author three further books, 'She Who Dares', 'Permission' and 'From the Ashes She is Ignited'.

Jo has worked in publishing since April 2018 and has supported over 500 authors with the interior design of their books, taking their manuscripts and converting them into quality interior files.

Jo set up Audio and Co.® to complement the formatting services she already offered enabling authors to record audiobooks and in 2021 extended these services out to podcast launches and management.

Jo is also the brains behind a simplified version of DMAIC continuous improvement for small business owners and entrepreneurs. Bringing the F*CK! toolkit and business support consultancy to market.

**F** - Find the issue/problem

**\*** - Understand it

**C** - Change it

**K** - KPIs to control it

**!** - Embed and Sustain it!

Jo is already busy working on her third solo book;

'How the F*CK!'

A no-nonsense guide, to planning, setting up and running your business.

## WHERE TO FIND AND CONTACT JO:

For Business Consultancy, Coaching, Service, Customer Experience, Continuous Improvement and access to the F*CK! Toolkit for business:

**Email:** jo@f-cktoolkit.co.uk

**Website:** https://f-cktoolkit.co.uk

**Linkedin:**

https://www.linkedin.com/company/89587237

―――――

For Audiobooks, Podcasts and Book Formatting Support;

**Email:** hello@audioandco.com

**Website:** https://audioandco.com

facebook.com/audioandco

instagram.com/audio_andco

tiktok.com/@audioandco

linkedin.com/company/89229806